Introduction

Goalkeeper warm-up shooting is essential for almost every training unit. These 60 warm-up shooting exercises provide you with a variety of ideas to make the warm-up shooting challenging and diverse, both for the goalkeepers and the field players. The exercises particularly focus on improving the players' dynamics even during the warm-up shooting.

The exercises are illustrated and described in an easy, comprehensible manner. They can be immediately integrated in every training unit. Whether you combine the exercises with additional coordination drills or use them as an introduction to the main part – various difficulty levels allow for adjustment of the warm-up shooting to each training unit and age group.

Sample figure:

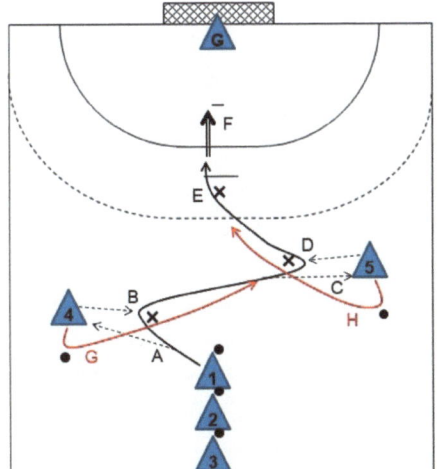

Running, passing, catching, and shooting

Publishing information
1st English edition released on 12 Okt 2018
German original edition released on 07 Jul 2015

Published by DV Concept
Editors, design, and layout: Jörg Madinger, Elke Lackner
Proofreading and English translation: Nina-Maria Nahlenz

ISBN: 978-3-95641-226-4

This publication is listed in the catalogue of the **German National Library**. Please refer to http://dnb.de for bibliographic data.

The work and its components are protected by copyright. No reprinting, photomechanical reproduction, storing or processing in electronic systems without the publisher's written permission.

Effective goalkeeper warm-up shooting
60 exercises for every handball training unit

Contents:

No.	Name	No.	2nd GK?	Difficulty level	Page
1	Warm-up shooting with two previous coordination exercises	7		☆	5
2	Simple series of shots with pass	7		☆	6
3	Quick back and forth drill	7		☆	7
4	Warm-up shooting from the back and wing positions	7		☆	8
5	Intense warm-up shooting exercise for the goalkeeper	9		☆	9
6	Piston movement with counter movement and subsequent shot	7		☆	10
7	Shot with subsequent team drill for the shooting players	9		☆	11
8	Warm-up shooting after moving around a player	9		☆	12
9	Warm-up shooting with piston movements	7		☆	13
10	Series of shots with previous running exercise	7		☆	14
11	Warm-up shooting with running and breaking away	7		☆	15
12	Series of shots with additional task	7		☆	16
13	Series of shots with speed drill for the goalkeeper	7		☆	17
14	Series of shots with quick changes of direction	7		☆	18
15	Series of shots with second pivot from the wing position	7		☆	19
16	Simple warm-up shooting with dribbling exercise	7		☆	20
17	Simple warm-up shooting combined with running moves	7		☆	21
18	Simple warm-up shooting in a small training group	5		☆	22
19	Running, passing, catching, and shooting	7		☆	23
20	Warm-up shooting with a subsequent shot at the opposite goal	8	X	☆	24
21	Intense warm-up shooting exercise for three goalkeepers	7	X	☆	25
22	Warm-up shooting with subsequent fast break initiation	8	X	☆	26
23	Warm-up shooting from the 6-meter line	10	X	☆	27
24	Double series of shots with additional coordination exercises	10	X	☆	28
25	Series of shots with additional task and pass	8	X	☆	29
26	Quick game opening and series of shots	8	X	☆	30
27	Series of shots over the entire court with piston movement	8	X	☆☆	31
28	Series of shots for the pivot from the 6-meter line	9		☆☆	32
29	Dynamic warm-up shooting with piston movement	10		☆☆	33
30	Quick warm-up shooting with subsequent fast break initiation and 2nd series of shots	7		☆☆	34
31	Quick back and forth, shot from the left/right wing position 1	7		☆☆	35

Effective goalkeeper warm-up shooting
60 exercises for every handball training unit

No.	Name	No	2nd GK?	Difficulty level	Page
32	Warm-up shooting at full speed 1	7		★★	36
33	Warm-up shooting at full speed 2	7		★★	37
34	Warm-up shooting at full speed 3	7		★★	38
35	Series of shots with a simple crossing move	7		★★	38
36	Quick back and forth, shot from the left/right wing position 2	7		★★	39
37	Warm-up shooting with crossing moves	9		★★	40
38	Series of shots with defense action	8		★★	41
39	Series of shots with parallel piston movement and defense	9		★★	42
40	Series of shots with piston movement/counter movement 1	9		★★	43
41	Series of shots with piston movement/counter movement 2	7		★★	44
42	Series of shots with piston movement/counter movement 3	7		★★	45
43	Series of shots with additional task for the goalkeeper 1	7		★★	46
44	Series of shots with additional task for the goalkeeper 2	7		★★	47
45	Series of shots with additional task for the goalkeeper 3	8	X	★★	48
46	Series of shots with additional task for the goalkeeper 4	8	X	★★	49
47	Series of shots with additional task for the goalkeeper 5	8		★★	50
48	Series of shots with additional task for the goalkeeper and the field players	7		★★	51
49	Series of shots with crossing moves and additional task for the goalkeeper	8		★★	52
50	Series of shots with dynamic running moves	7		★★	53
51	Warm-up shooting for two goalkeepers at one goal	8	X	★★	54
52	Saving banana shots and initiating fast breaks	10	X	★★	55
53	Series of shots and fast break initiation with coordination exercise	8	X	★★	56
54	Fast break initiation plus series of shots	10	X	★★	57
55	Series of 4 shots with subsequent fast break 1	8	X	★★	58
56	Series of 4 shots with subsequent fast break 2	8	X	★★	60
57	Warm-up shooting at full speed 4	8		★★★	62
58	Series of shots with piston movement/counter movement 4	7	X	★★★	63
59	Series of shots with coordination exercise for goalkeepers and field players	8	X	★★★	64
60	Series of shots with subsequent fast break initiation	8	X	★★★	65

About the editor

Further reference books published by DV Concept

Effective goalkeeper warm-up shooting
60 exercises for every handball training unit

Key:

No. of exercise   Name of exercise   Minimum number of players

No. 9	Warm-up shooting with piston movements	7	⭐
Equipment required:	7 cones, ball box with sufficient number of handballs		

Difficulty level
Easy: ⭐
Medium: ⭐⭐
Difficult: ⭐⭐⭐

✕	Cone
 ▬	Small gym mat
 ⠿	Ball box
 ▢	Small vaulting box
▬▬	Balance bench
 ○	Hoop
 —	Foam noodles (foam beams)
●	Balloon

Effective goalkeeper warm-up shooting
60 exercises for every handball training unit

No. 1	Warm-up shooting with two previous coordination exercises	7	
Equipment required:	6-8 hoops, 5-8 foam beams, 2 cones, sufficient number of handballs		

Course:

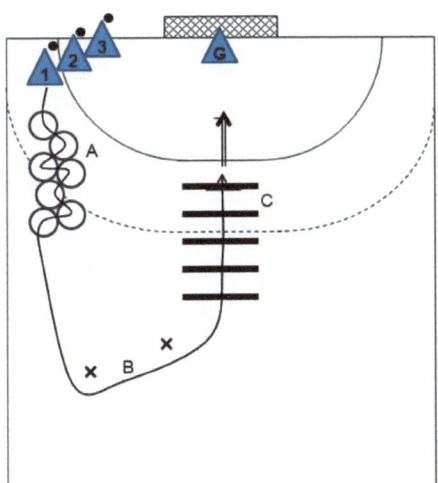

- ① starts with quick steps, touching the ground only one time per hoop (A).
- Afterwards, ① sprints around the cones (B) and towards the foam beams. He runs through the line of foam beams with one double-step (left foot/right foot) per interspace.
- Afterwards, ① shoots at the goal as instructed (top, middle, bottom).
- ② starts the same course a bit delayed.

Variant:
- Position the hoops in a different order again and again.
- Change the number of floor contacts between the foam beams, but keep the running flow.

⚠ The players should time their moves in such a way that there is a quick series of shots for the goalkeeper.

No. 2	Simple series of shots with pass	7	★
Equipment required:	Sufficient number of handballs		

Course:

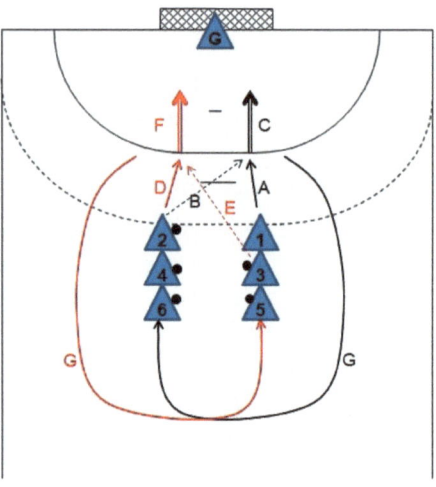

- 1 starts to approach the goal without a ball (A) and receives a pass from 2 (B).
- 1 shoots at the right side of the goal as instructed (hands, top, bottom) and from within the corridor (C).
- 2 starts to approach the goal (D) and receives a pass from 3 into his running path (E).
- 2 shoots at the left side of the goal as instructed and from within the corridor (F).
- And so on.
- After the shot, the players each quickly fetch a ball and line up on the other side (G).

⚠ Define the distance between the two rows according to the players' level of performance.

⚠ The players should time their moves in such a way that there is a continuous series of shots for the goalkeeper.

Effective goalkeeper warm-up shooting
60 exercises for every handball training unit

No. 3	Quick back and forth drill	7	★
Equipment required:	Sufficient number of handballs		

Course:
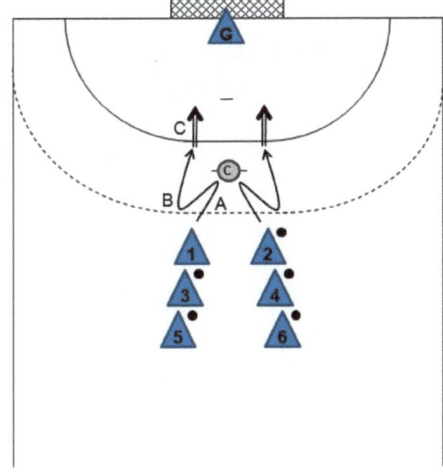

- The coach stands at the 7-meter line and stretches out his hands.
- ① does 2-3 quick steps forward and hits the coach's palms (A). Afterwards, ① immediately moves back 2-3 steps (B) in order to do a dynamic forward piston movement and to shoot at the left side of the goal as instructed (top, middle, bottom), approx. from the 7-meter line (C).
- ② starts the same course a bit delayed, does a forward piston movement on the right side, and shoots at the right side of the goal.

Variants:
- Jump shot.
- Shooting with the wrong foot in front.

No. 4	Warm-up shooting from the back and wing positions	7	★
Equipment required:	4 cones, sufficient number of handballs (ball box with spare balls)		

Course:

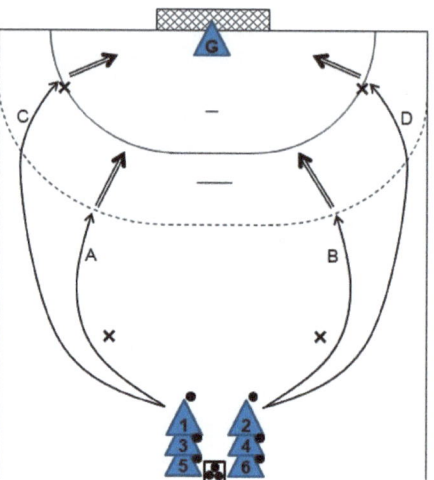

- All players stand at the center line, each of them holding a ball.
- **1** starts and runs around the cone on the left, dynamically approaches (A) the 9-meter line, and shoots at the goal as instructed (top, middle, bottom).
- **2** starts a bit delayed, runs (B) around the cone on the right, approaches the 9-meter line, and shoots at the goal.
- And so on.
- The players who shot at the goal, quickly line up at the center line again and pick up a ball from the ball box.
- Repeat the drill until no handballs are left.

Variant:

- **1** starts and runs around the cone on the left, runs (C) along the far left side of the playing field until he has reached the left wing position, and finally shoots from there. **2** starts a bit delayed and runs along the far right side (D).

Shooting variants:

- Jump shot.
- Shooting with the wrong foot in front.

Effective goalkeeper warm-up shooting
60 exercises for every handball training unit

No. 5	Intense warm-up shooting exercise for the goalkeeper	9	★
Equipment required:	Sufficient number of handballs		

Course:
- The players stand face-to-face in order to create a lane (keep a distance of approx. 2 meters between 1 and 2, and approx. 1/2 meter between 1 and 3).
- The players each hold their handball in both hands, in such a way that the goalkeeper can reach it.
- The goalkeeper G quickly sidesteps through the lane (A) and touches each handball with one hand.
- G should return to his basic arm posture again and again while sidestepping from player to player.
- As soon as G has run through the lane, G moves to the goal (B), the players start approaching the goal dynamically (C), and do a series of shots at the goal as instructed (top, middle, bottom).

Variants:
- Shooting with the wrong foot in front.
- Jump shot.
- Underarm shot.

No. 6	Piston movement with counter movement and subsequent shot	7	★
Equipment required:	4 cones, sufficient number of handballs		

Course:

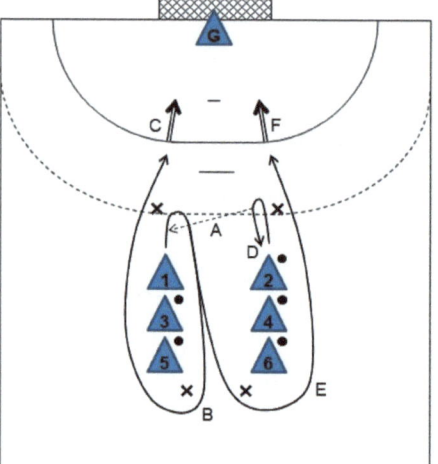

- 1 does the piston movement and receives a pass into his running path from 2, who also does the piston movement (A).
- 1 immediately takes a turn towards the inner side, dribbles around the backmost cone (B), dribbles towards the goal, and eventually shoots at the left side of the goal as instructed (top, middle, bottom) (C).
- 2 moves backward to his initial position immediately after playing the pass (D), does a forward piston movement again, receives a pass from 3 into his running path, also runs around his group, and shoots at the goal as instructed.
- And so on.

Variant:

- 1 diagonally runs around the backmost cone of the other group (E) and shoots at the goal (F).

⚠ The players should time their action in such a way that there is a smooth rhythm for the goalkeeper.

Effective goalkeeper warm-up shooting
60 exercises for every handball training unit

No. 7	Shot with subsequent team drill for the shooting players	9	★
Equipment required:	1 balance bench, sufficient number of handballs		

Setting:
- Position a balance bench upside down on the floor (seating surface on the floor).

Course:
- Right before each shooting round, the coach defines a task which has to be done on the bench.
- ①　starts with a ball (A) and shoots at the left side of the goal as instructed (hands, top, bottom) (B).
- ②　starts a bit delayed with a ball (C) and shoots at the right side of the goal as instructed (D).

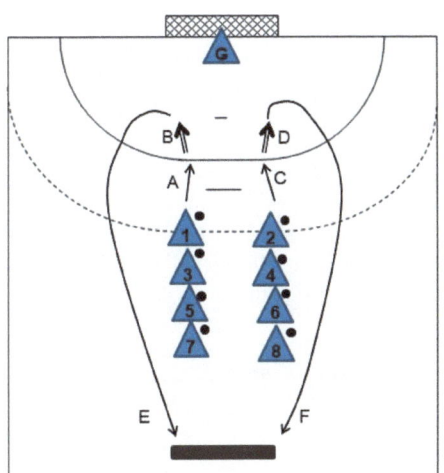

- After the shot, ① (E) and ② (F) sprint to the bench.
- After the shooting round, all the shooting players must stand on the bench according to the coach's task. While doing so, the players who already shot at the goal should organize themselves ideally, in such a way that they do not have to change their position anymore once they stand on the bench.
- After the last shot, the goalkeeper also sprints to the bench and is the last player trying to get into the right position.
- If the players need to switch positions one more time, they should solve this situation without a player having to leave the bench.
- Afterwards, the players start the next shooting round with a new task.

Tasks for players on the bench:
- Form a line sorted by height.
- By alphabetical order of first names.
- By age.
- By chronological order of birthdays, beginning in January.

Effective goalkeeper warm-up shooting
60 exercises for every handball training unit

No. 8	Warm-up shooting after moving around a player	9	★
Equipment required:	1 cone, sufficient number of handballs		

Course:

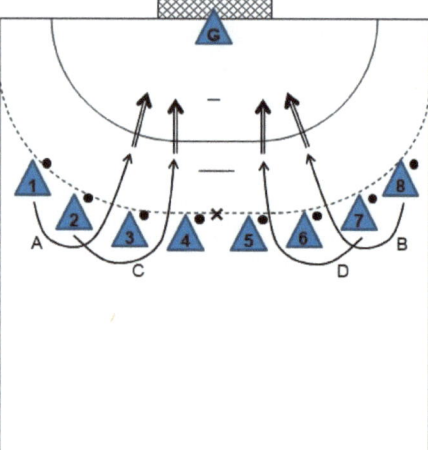

- **1** runs around **2** (A), dribbles towards the goal, and shoots as instructed.
- **8** starts a bit delayed, runs around **7** (B), dribbles towards the goal, and shoots at the goal as instructed (top, middle, bottom).
- **2** starts immediately after **1** has shot, and runs around **3** (C).
- **7** starts immediately after **8** has shot, and runs around **6** (D).
- **4** and **5** are the last players; they run around the cone and shoot at the goal.

Variants:
- Jump shot.
- Shooting with the wrong foot in front.

⚠ The players should time their action in such a way that there is a smooth rhythm for the goalkeeper.

No. 9	Warm-up shooting with piston movements	7	★
Equipment required:	7 cones, ball box with sufficient number of handballs		

Course:

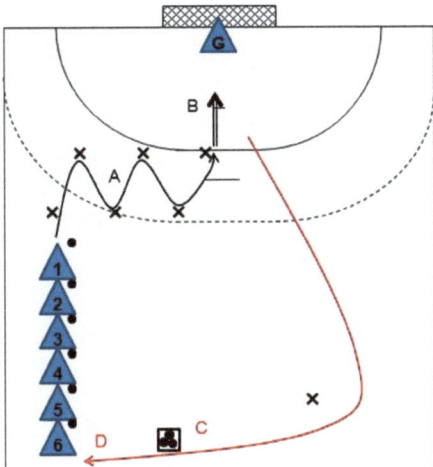

- **1** starts with a ball, runs dynamically back and forth (viewing direction towards the goal) from cone to cone (A), and eventually shoots at the goal as instructed (top, middle, bottom) (B).
- After the shot, **1** immediately runs around the backmost cone, picks up a new ball (C), and lines up again (D).
- **2** immediately starts after **1**, in order to create a smooth rhythm for **G**.
- Repeat the course until there is no ball left in the box.

Variants:

- Sidestepping from cone to cone.
- Shooting with the wrong foot in front.

⚠ The players should time their action in such a way that there is a smooth rhythm for the goalkeeper.

No. 10	Series of shots with previous running exercise	7	★
Equipment required:	8 cones, sufficient number of handballs		

Course:

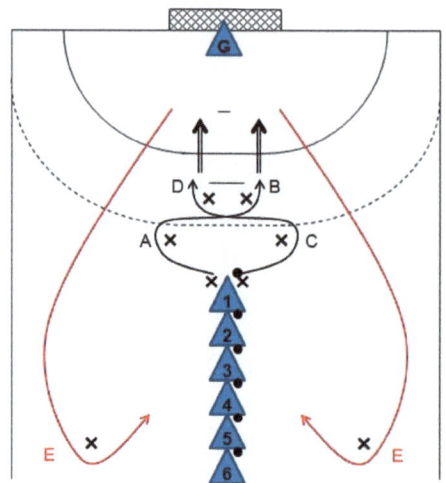

- 1 starts sidestepping quickly to the left, runs around the cone (A), quickly moves to the right, runs around the cone on the right side (B), and shoots at the (right side of the) goal from within the corridor.
- 2 starts a bit delayed (so that the goalkeeper faces a series of shots), quickly sidesteps around the cone on the right side (C), quickly moves to the left, runs around the cone on the left (D), and shoots at the (left side of) the goal from within the corridor.
- And so on.
- After the shot, the players each sprint around the backmost cone (E) before fetching their ball quickly.

Variant:
- Jump shot (at level of the cones).

Effective goalkeeper warm-up shooting
60 exercises for every handball training unit

No. 11	Warm-up shooting with running and change of direction	7	★
Equipment required:	6 cones, ball box with sufficient number of handballs		

Course:

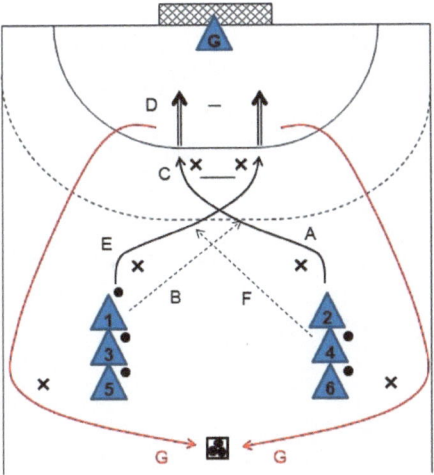

- 2 runs around the cone (A) and then diagonally to the left.
- 1 passes the ball into the running path of 2 (B).
- 2 runs around the cone on the left (C) and shoots at the left side of the goal as instructed (D).
- 1 immediately starts after playing the pass to 2 (B), runs around the cone (E) and then diagonally to the right.
- 4 passes the ball into the running path of 1 (F), and 1 shoots at the right side of the goal as instructed.
- After the shot, the players immediately sprint around the backmost cone, towards the ball box, pick up a new ball, and line up again (G).
- Repeat the course until there is no ball left in the box.

⚠ The players should time their action in such a way that there is a smooth rhythm for the goalkeeper.

No. 12	Series of shots with additional task	7	★
Equipment required:	2 cones, 2 small gym mats, ball box with sufficient number of handballs		

Course:

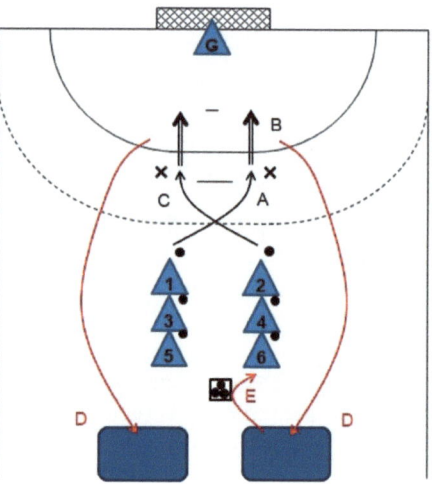

-  has a ball, runs diagonally to the right (A), and shoots at the right side of the goal as instructed (hands, top, bottom, middle), and from within the corridor (B).
- 2 starts a bit delayed, runs diagonally to the left, and shoots at the left side of the goal as instructed, and from within the corridor (C).
- After the shot, the shooting players dynamically run to the small gym mat where they do a somersault (D).
- Afterwards, they pick up a ball and line up again (E).
- Each player should shoot at least two times, in order to create a long series of shots for the goalkeeper.

Variants:
- The players do a handstand on the mat.
- The players do a backward somersault on the mat.

Effective goalkeeper warm-up shooting
60 exercises for every handball training unit

No. 13	Series of shots with speed drill for the goalkeeper	7	★
Equipment required:	1 Deuser band, ball box with sufficient number of handballs		

Initial position:
- The goalkeeper stands in the center of the goal, about half a meter in front of the goal line, with the Deuser band around his hips.
- The coach stands next to him and holds him at the Deuser band.

Course:
- 1 approaches the goal with the ball and shoots at the left top corner of the goal (A).
- G should react dynamically and try to save the shot (B). The coach behind him pulls him back at the Deuser band in order to make it more difficult for him to move.
- After the shot, 1 makes a sprint to the ball box and lines up again with a ball (C).
- As soon as G stands in the initial position in the center again, 2 shoots at the goal.
- And so on.

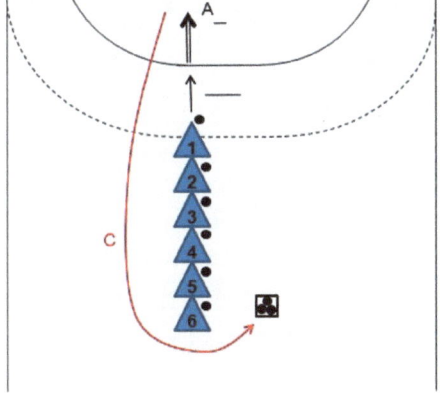

Variants:
- Shots at the bottom corners of the goal.
- Shots at the top and bottom corners of the goal alternately.
- The coach stands behind the goalkeeper and holds him at the Deuser band; now the shooting players may shoot at the left and right side of the goal alternately (top, middle).

⚠ Pull the Deuser band in such a way that G may save the shot smoothly but nevertheless must overcome the resistance.

⚠ The players should adjust the series of shots to the speed of G.

No. 14	Series of shots with quick changes of direction	7	★
Equipment required:	1 cone, sufficient number of handballs		

Course:

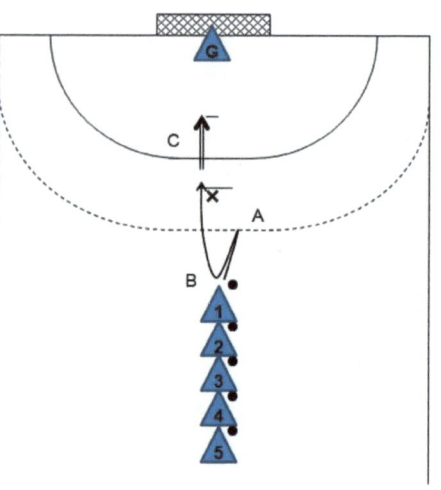

- **1** dynamically runs forward and steps on the 9-meter line with one foot (A).
- **1** runs back again immediately and exchanges a high-five with **2**, who stretches out his hand (B).
- Afterwards, **1** runs past the cone and eventually shoots at the goal as instructed (C).
- After exchanging the high-five, **2** immediately runs forward, also steps on the 9-meter line (A); and so on.

Variant:
- The players do the same course but shoot from the right side of the cone.
- The players shoot with the wrong foot in front; jump shot.

⚠ Make sure the players run back and forth at high speed.

| No. 15 | Series of shots with second pivot from the wing position | 7 | |

Equipment required: 4 cones, sufficient number of handballs

Course:

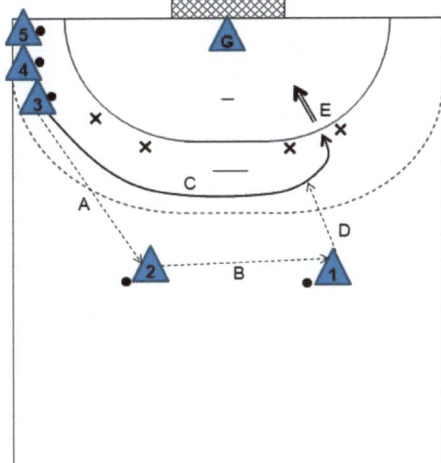

- Two players stand on the left and right back position. Each of them has a ball lying on the floor next to them.
- 3 passes to 2 (A), 2 passes to 1 (B).
- Once 2 has passed the ball to 1 (B), 3 starts and quickly runs a curve along the 6-meter line (C). 1 passes the ball to 3 (D).
- 3 runs through the cones and shoots at the goal as instructed (hands, top, bottom) (E).
- As soon as 2 has passed the ball to 1 (B), he receives a pass from 4, and repeats the course.
- Once as all the players on the wing position have run past 2, 2 picks up his ball, plays a pass to 1, receives a return pass, runs through the cones, and shoots at the goal as instructed.
- 1 then picks up his ball, runs through the cones, and shoots at the goal as instructed.

⚠ Change the back position players regularly.

⚠ Start the course from the left and right side alternately.

⚠ The players should pass the ball in a smooth manner in order to create a series of shots for the goalkeeper.

Effective goalkeeper warm-up shooting
60 exercises for every handball training unit

No. 16	Simple warm-up shooting with dribbling exercise	7	★
Equipment required:	12 cones, sufficient number of handballs		

Course:

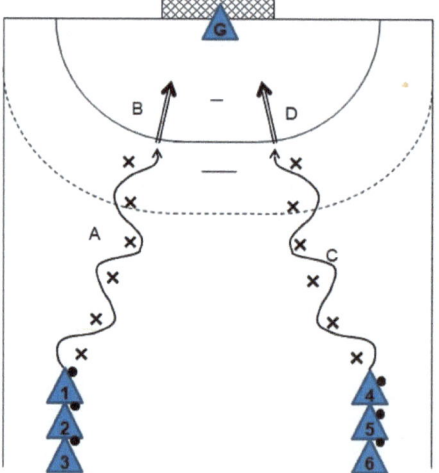

- 1 starts with a ball, dribbles around the cones (A), and shoots at (the left side of) the goal as instructed (hands, top, bottom), and from within the corridor (B).

- Once 1 has arrived the third cone, 4 starts the course on the other side, dribbles around the cones (C), and shoots at (the right side of) the goal as instructed, and from within the corridor (D).

- Once 4 has arrived the third cone, 2 starts; and so on.

⚠ The players should stay in sufficient distance to each other so that each of them is able to dribble around the cones quickly and without getting into each other's way.

⚠ The goalkeeper should face a series of shots.

⚠ The players should change their hands when dribbling (shield off the ball with the body).

Effective goalkeeper warm-up shooting
60 exercises for every handball training unit

No. 17	Simple warm-up shooting combined with running moves	7	★
Equipment required:	2 cones, sufficient number of handballs		

Course:

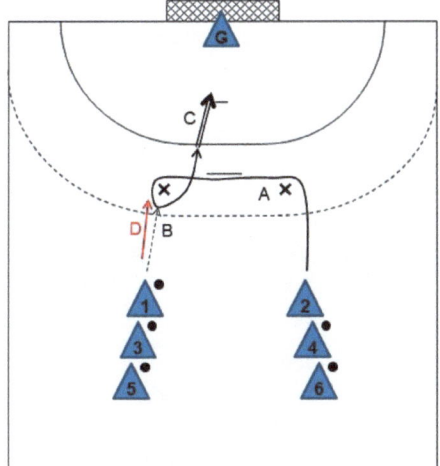

- 2 starts without a ball, runs around both cones (A), and receives a pass from 1 (B).
- 2 now approaches the goal with the ball, and eventually shoots as instructed (top, middle, bottom) (C).
- Once he has passed the ball to 2 (B), 1 immediately starts running to the right, around both cones (D), and receives a pass from 4; and so on.
- Between the shots, G does 2-3 quick jumping jacks on the spot.

⚠ The players should run around the cones at top speed; the running direction is irrelevant, however.

No. 18	Simple warm-up shooting in a small training group	5	★
Equipment required:	Ball box with sufficient number of handballs		

Setting:
- Put a ball box with nine handballs (three balls per player) in the center.

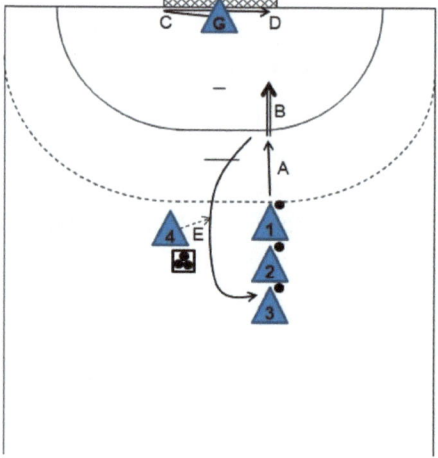

Course:
- **1** starts with a ball, runs forward (A), and shoots at the right side of the goal as instructed (top, middle, bottom) (B).
- **G** starts from the center of the goal, dynamically sidesteps to the left, touches the goalpost (C), dynamically sidesteps back again, and saves (D) the ball shot by **1** at the right side of the goal (B). Afterwards, **G** immediately goes back to his initial position, the center of the goal.
- **2** starts a bit delayed, so that **G** faces a series of shots and yet is able to do the moves (sidestepping) correctly.
- After the shot, **1** immediately moves back and to the side, receives a pass from **4** (E), and lines up again.
- As soon as each player has shot four times, change the feeder (**4**), and repeat the series with another instruction (top, middle, bottom).

⚠ The series is most suitable for 2-3 shooting players. After their shot, the players each must line up again immediately with a new ball.

Effective goalkeeper warm-up shooting
60 exercises for every handball training unit

No. 19	Running, passing, catching, and shooting	7	★
Equipment required:	3 cones, sufficient number of handballs		

Course:

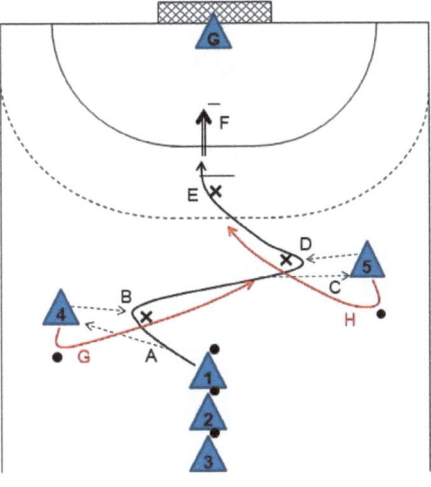

- 1 starts with a ball, passes it to 4 (A), and immediately receives a return pass (B). While doing this, 1 runs around the cone.
- Afterwards, 1 immediately takes a turn, passes the ball to 5 (C), and receives a return pass at once (D). 1 runs around both cones (E) and eventually shoots at the goal as instructed (F).
- 2 starts the same course a bit delayed; and so on.
- Once all the players have shot, 4 immediately picks up his ball (G), runs around the cone, plays a double pass with 5, and shoots at the goal.
- As soon as 4 has finished his action, 5 immediately picks up his ball, runs around the two cones, and also shoots at the goal (H).

⚠ Make sure the players always do the running and passing moves at high speed.

⚠ The players should change the directions between the cones in a quick and dynamic manner.

No. 20	Warm-up shooting with a subsequent shot at the opposite goal	8	★
Equipment required:	Sufficient number of handballs (spare balls at the left and right side of the goal)		

Course:

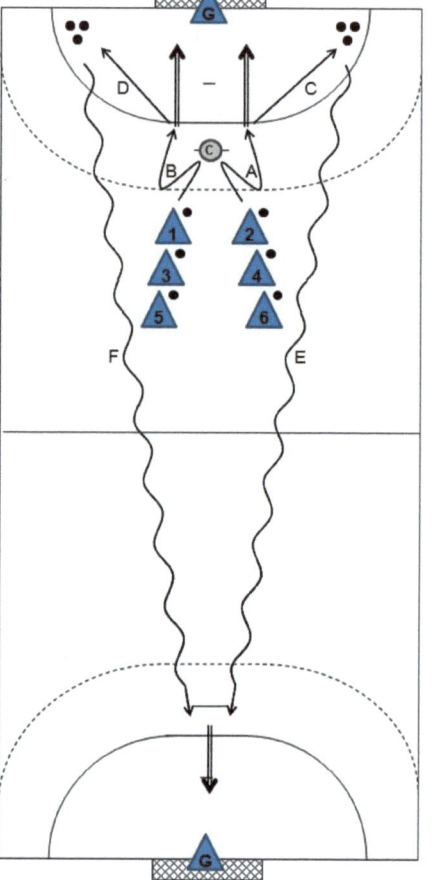

- The coach stands at the 7-meter line and stretches out his hands.
- ① does 2-3 quick steps forward and hits the coach's palms. Afterwards, he immediately moves back 2-3 steps in order to do a dynamic forward piston movement and to shoot at the left side of the goal as instructed (top, middle, bottom), approx. from the 7-meter line and from within the corridor (B).
- ② starts the same course a bit delayed (A) and shoots at the right side of the goal.
- Once ① has shot, ① (D) sprints to the spare balls lying in the field right in front of the goal line, picks up a ball, and starts to run a fast break towards the opposite goal (F).
- ② starts the same course a bit delayed (C and E).

Series of shots:
- Goal #1: Hands, top, bottom, middle.
- Goal #2 (at top speed): Hands and feet, top, bottom, middle alternately.

The goalkeepers remain in their respective goal throughout a series of shots; afterwards, they change goals.

Variants:
- Jump shot.
- Shooting with the wrong foot in front.

Effective goalkeeper warm-up shooting
60 exercises for every handball training unit

No. 21	Intense warm-up shooting exercise for three goalkeepers	7	
Equipment required:	Two handballs per player		

Setting:
- In the beginning, each player has two handballs.
- The three goalkeepers stand in the goal (G) and next to the goal (G1 and G2), as shown in the figure.

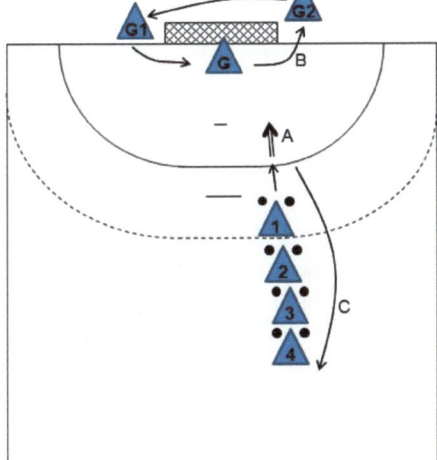

Course:
- 1 starts and shoots (A) at the goal as instructed (top, middle, bottom).
- G saves the shot. Afterwards, the goalkeepers move to the respective next position (rotation) (B).
- 2 should time the next shot in such a way that G1 is able to position himself in the center of the goal before 2 shoots at the goal.
- After the shot, the shooting players quickly move to the side and run backward in order to line up again (B).

⚠ The players should adapt their speed in such a way that the goalkeepers are able to stand and start from the center of the goal to save the shot (i.e. they should not be forced to run).

No. 22	Warm-up shooting with subsequent fast break initiation	8	
Equipment required:	Sufficient number of handballs		

Basic setting:
- The players evenly line up around the 6-meter line, each holding a handball.

Course:
- 1 starts the series of shots and shoots at the long corner (A) as instructed (top, middle, bottom).
- The other players shoot at the short (B) and long corners alternately.
- Once the last player (6) has shot, 1 starts a fast break. As fast as possible, the goalkeeper fetches one of the balls shot at the goal (C) and initiates the fast break (D).
- 1 shoots a jump shot from the 9-meter line (E).
- The other players do the same course.

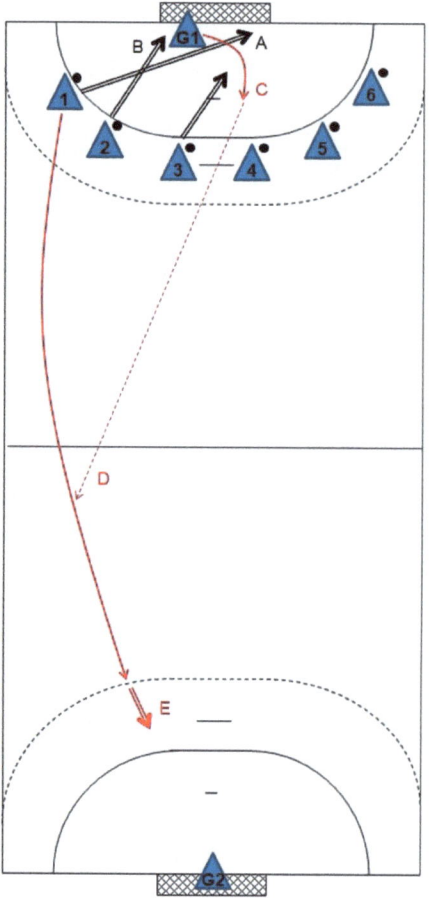

⚠ During the first series of shots (from the 6-meter line), G1 should slowly move along in a semicircle with the shooting players in order to keep the ideal position.

⚠ Put some spare balls on the floor next to the goal in case some of the balls shot before are outside of the 6-meter zone.

Effective goalkeeper warm-up shooting
60 exercises for every handball training unit

No. 23	Warm-up shooting from the 6-meter line	10	★
Equipment required:	Sufficient number of handballs		

Setting:
- The players line up between the 6- and 9-meter line, each holding a handball.

Course:
- **1** starts from the wing position. At the beginning, **G1** stands slightly closer to the center of the goal.
- **1** shoots the ball top left (A); the goalkeeper **G1** makes a small step to the right and tries to save the ball (B).
- **2** then shoots top right, a bit delayed (C). The players must not shoot into the goal corners; the goalkeeper **G1** must be able to save the shots with only a small step (D).
- **3** then shoots top left again, a bit delayed (E). At the end of the series of 4 shots, **4** shoots top right (F).
- After he has shot, **4** runs a fast break at once (G).
- **G1** immediately fetches a ball after the 4th shot, goes into a good throwing position (H) (diagonal pass), and then passes the ball into the running path of **4** (J).
- **4** shoots without being interrupted (K).
- Afterwards, the next group of 4 (**5**, **6**, **7**, and **8**) starts the same course on the right side.

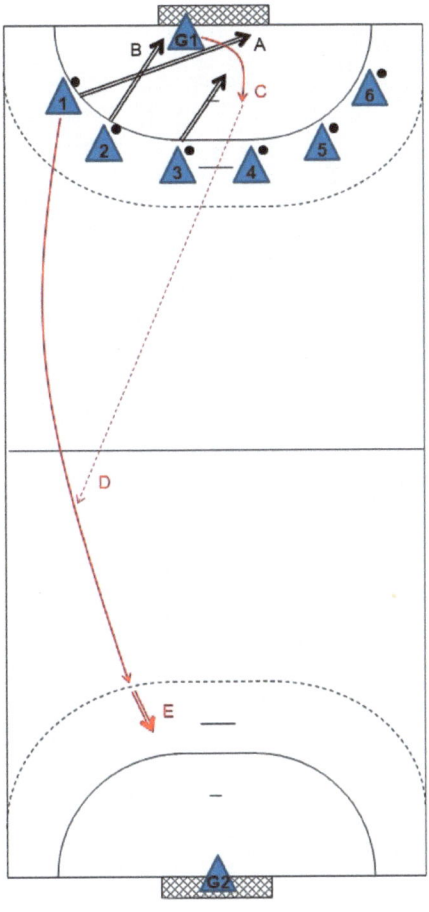

⚠ During the series of 4 shots, the players need to make sure that the goalkeeper **G1** can move from shot to shot in the most optimal way. The goalkeeper **G1** should be able to save the shots using a proper technique.

No. 24	Double series of shots with additional coordination exercises	10	★
Equipment required:	5 foam beams, 6 hoops, sufficient number of handballs		

Course:

1 and 5 start simultaneously:

- **Group #1:** The players each quickly step (left and right foot) between the foam beams (A), and then shoot at the goal as instructed (hands, top, bottom, middle). Afterwards, the players immediately fetch their ball and sprint to the other half of the court (C).
- **Group #2:** The players each run through the line of hoops as fast as possible with one quick step per hoop (B), and then shoot at the goal as instructed. Afterwards, the players immediately fetch their ball and sprint to the other half of the court (C).
- Both groups should follow the same instructions when shooting at the goal (i.e. top, middle, bottom).

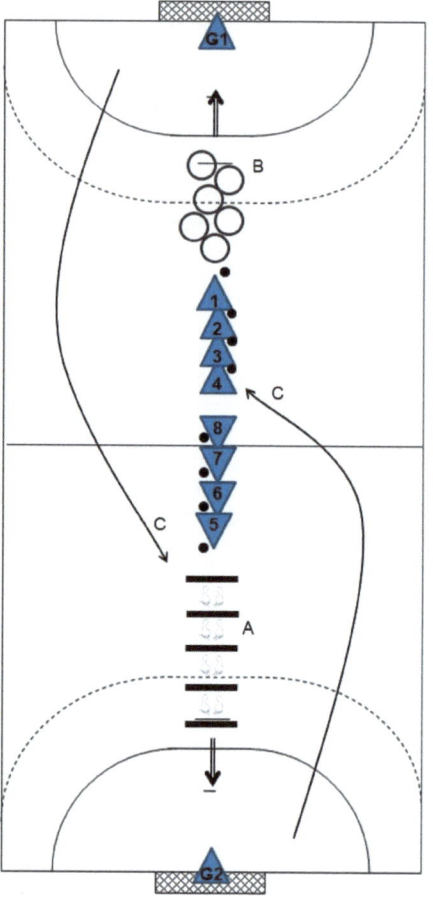

Variants:

- Jump with both feet or with one foot (left and right). Change the shooting instructions after each round.

⚠ The players should run through the lines of hoops and foam beams in such a way that there is a smooth rhythm for the goalkeeper.

Effective goalkeeper warm-up shooting
60 exercises for every handball training unit

No. 25	Series of shots with additional task and pass	8	★
Equipment required:	7 hoops, 1 cone, sufficient number of handballs		

Course:

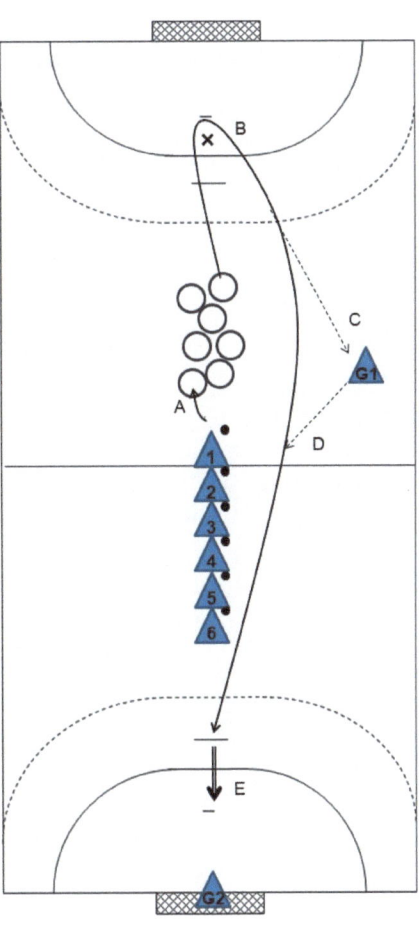

- ▲1 starts with a ball and runs through the line of hoops as instructed (A).
- After the last hoop, he sprints around the cone (B) and passes the ball to ▲G1 (C).
- ▲1 immediately receives a return pass (D), quickly runs to the other half of the court, and shoots as instructed (top, middle, bottom) (E).
- ▲2 should start immediately after ▲1 so that there is a smooth rhythm for ▲G2.
- And so on.

⚠ When starting to approach the goal (E), the players should keep a certain distance in order to create a quick warm-up shooting round for ▲G2.

Instructions for running though the line of hoops:

- One step per hoop (left-right-left...)
- Two steps per hoop (left and right-left and right...)
- While running, throw the ball in the air and catch it.
- While running, move the ball around the hips in circles.

Effective goalkeeper warm-up shooting
60 exercises for every handball training unit

No. 26	Quick game opening and series of shots	8	★
Equipment required:	Sufficient number of handballs		

Course:

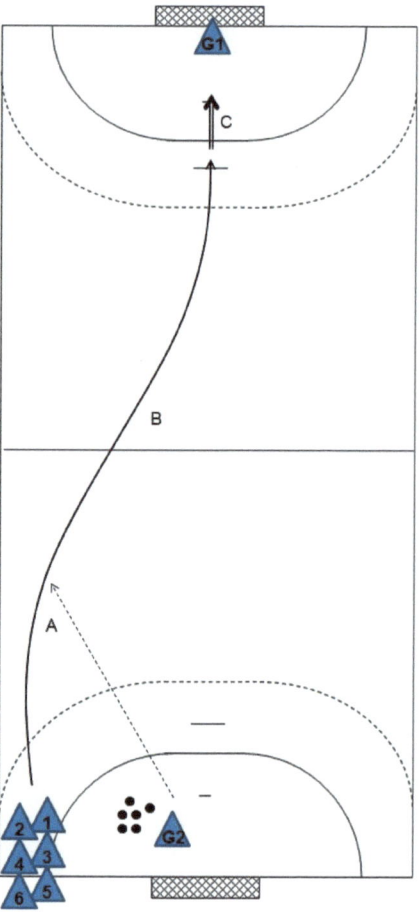

- 1 starts and immediately receives a pass from G2 into his running path (A).
- 1 sprints to the center line (B), slows down a bit, and waits for the other players.
- Immediately after 1 has started and received the ball from G2, 2 starts and also receives a ball from G2 into his running path.
- Repeat until each player has received a ball.
- The players shoot at the goal (C) as instructed, in such a way that G1 faces a series of shots (hands, top, bottom, middle).
- After the series of shots, the players repeat the course on the other side. G1 passes the ball, G2 should save the series of shots, etc.

Variants:

- Shooting with the wrong foot in front.
- Jump shot.

⚠ This exercise is very intense, also for the goalkeeper playing the passes. He should pass the ball as fast as possible, but nevertheless precisely to avoid long waiting periods for the shooting players.

No. 27	Series of shots over the entire court with piston movement	8	
Equipment required:	1 cone, ball box with sufficient number of handballs		

Course:

- 1 and 2 start simultaneously and pass a ball three times while running (A, B, and C). The players should organize their running and passing moves in such a way that 2 plays the last pass to 1 behind the cone (C).
- 1 dribbles towards the goal and shoots (E) as instructed.
- 2 stops running forward, dynamically runs around the cone, and receives a pass from G2 into his running path (D).
- 2 dribbles towards the goal and shoots (E) as instructed.
- The next group of players should start a bit delayed, in such a way that the goalkeeper faces a series of shots.
- And so on.
- After the shot, the shooting players each sprint to the other half of the court, and afterwards pick up a new ball (F).

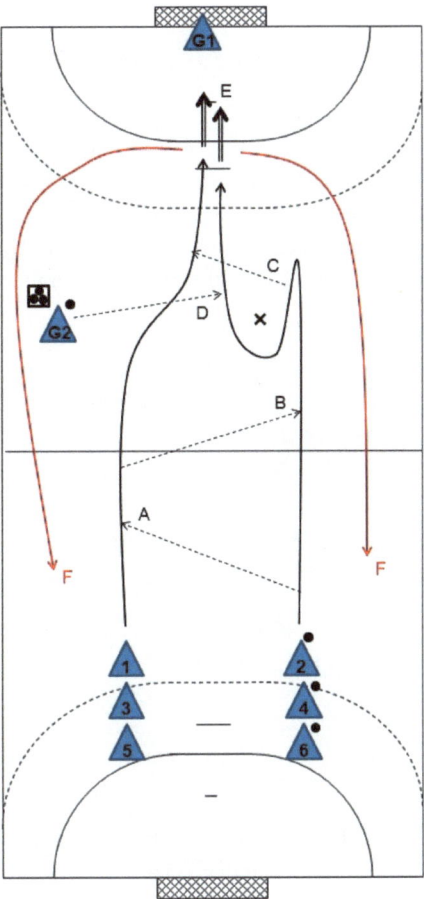

No. 28	Series of shots for the pivot from the 6-meter line	9	★★
Equipment required:	4 cones, 2 foam noodles (foam beams), 2 ball boxes with sufficient number of handballs		

Course:

- 2 does a piston movement while receiving the pass from 1 into his running path (A).
- While holding the ball, 2 dynamically moves towards the inner side, runs around the two cones (B), and passes the ball to 1 at the 6-meter line (C).
- 1 makes a step forward, picks up the ball, and shoots at the left side of the goal as instructed (top, middle, bottom) (D).
- The players on the other side start the course a bit delayed and shoot at the right side of the goal (E) so that G faces a series of shots.
- Following the action, 1 and 2 line up again (F and G). 2 picks up a ball from the ball box, etc.

Variant:
- The pass to the pivot (C) should be played as a jump shot pass.

⚠ The back position players (2 and 3) should move towards the inner side without dribbling, if possible (i.e. observe the three-step rule).

No. 29	Dynamic warm-up shooting with piston movement	10	★★
Equipment required:	8 cones, sufficient number of handballs		

Preparation:
- The players each have a ball and line up on the right and left side behind the cones. One player (9) stands in the center without a ball.

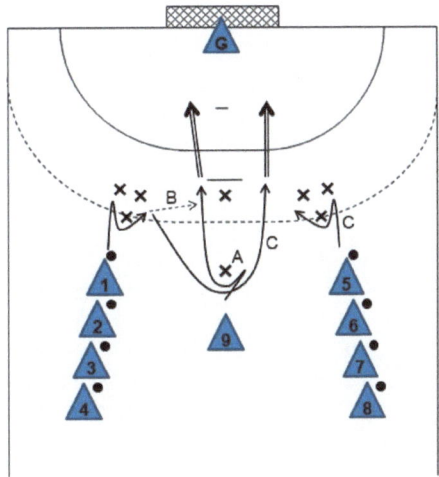

Course:
- 1 does a dynamic body feint in front of the cone while holding the ball.
- 9 starts in parallel, does a body feint, runs to the left (A), and receives a pass from 1 afterwards (B).
- 9 makes a stem shot at the goal as instructed (top, middle, bottom).
- After playing the pass to 9, 1 quickly sidesteps backward around the backmost cone in the center (C).
- 5 starts the same course as 1, a bit delayed and inversely, however. 5 makes a body feint in front of the cone, moves towards the inner side, and passes the ball to 1 who approaches him from the back.

Variants:
- The players should increase their speed continuously.
- The players shoot a jump shot.

No. 30	Quick warm-up shooting with subsequent fast break initiation and 2nd series of shots	7	
Equipment required:	2 cones, sufficient number of handballs		

Course:

- The players shoot at the short and long corner alternately as instructed (hands, top, middle, bottom) (A).
- After the shot, they sprint to a predefined line behind the center line (B).
- During the series of shots, the goalkeeper should follow the shooting player's position (C) in order to adjust the angle ideally.
- As soon as each player has shot, the goalkeeper runs to the first ball (D) and plays a long pass to 1 (F), then runs to the next ball (E), etc., until each player has a ball again.
- 6 starts, runs through the cones, and shoots at the goal as instructed before (G).
- The other players start a bit delayed in order to create a series of shots for the goalkeeper.

Variant:

- Two goalkeepers passing the balls and saving the shots alternately.

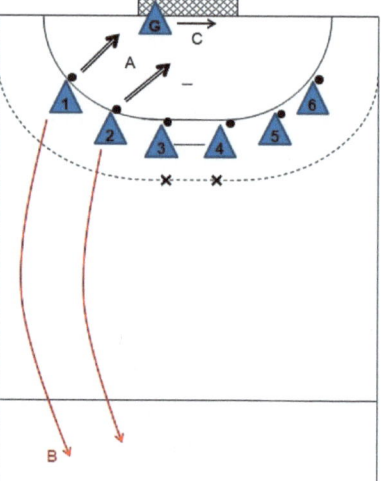

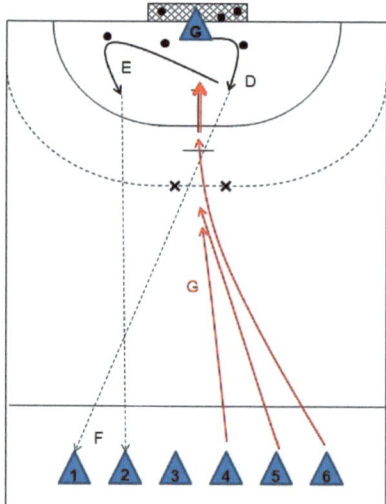

No. 31	Quick back and forth, shot from the left/right wing position 1	7	
Equipment required:	6 cones, sufficient number of handballs		

Course:

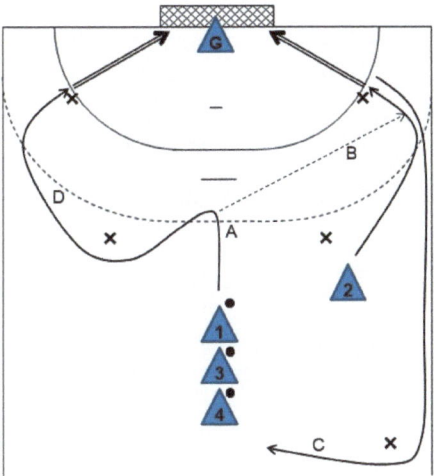

- 1 does a piston movement (A) and passes the ball (B) into the running path of 2 who shoots from the right wing position.
- Following the shot 2 runs a curve, sprints to the center line (C), and lines up again.
- 1 immediately moves backward to the left and runs around the two cones on the left side (D).
- 3 does a piston movement and passes the ball into the running path of 1 who shoots from the left wing position.
- And so on.

⚠ The goalkeeper should be given sufficient time to get into the correct basic position in order to save the shot from the wing player.

Effective goalkeeper warm-up shooting
60 exercises for every handball training unit

No. 32	Warm-up shooting at full speed 1	7	★★
Equipment required:	2 cones, sufficient number of handballs		

Course:

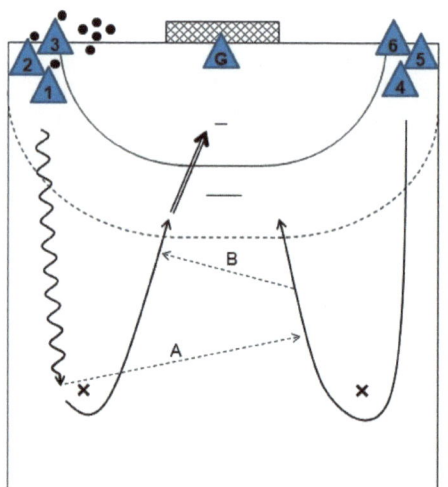

- 1 and 4 start simultaneously, with 1 dribbling the ball.
- Both run around the cone.
- Immediately after they have surrounded the cone, 1 passes the ball (A) to 4 who immediately plays a return pass (B).
- The players shoot at the goal alternately and as instructed (top, middle, bottom) (e.g. top left/right).
- The second group should start a bit delayed, so that there is a smooth rhythm for the goalkeeper.

Variants:

- Jump shot.
- Shooting with the wrong foot in front.

| No. 33 | Warm-up shooting at full speed 2 | 7 | ★★ |

Equipment required: 2 cones, sufficient number of handballs

Course:

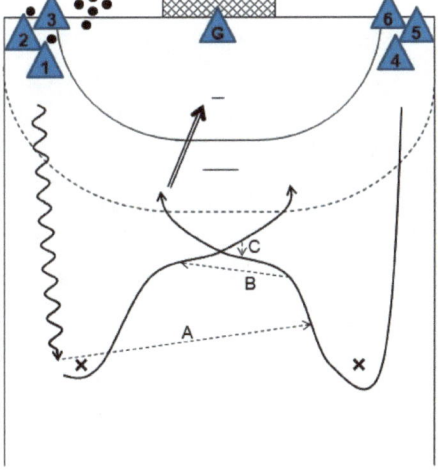

- 1 and 4 start simultaneously, with 1 dribbling the ball.
- Both run around the cone.
- Immediately after they have surrounded the cone, 1 passes the ball (A) to 4.
- 1 immediately receives a return pass (B) and starts a crossing move.
- 4 crosses behind him and receives a pass from 1 (C).
- The players shoot alternately and as instructed (top, middle, bottom).
- The second group should start a bit delayed, so that there is a smooth rhythm for the goalkeeper.

Variants:
- Jump shot.
- Shooting with the wrong foot in front.
- Jump shot pass (drop the ball in the air on the back side during the crossing).
- Handballs on the other side -> The players do the same course inversely.

No. 34	Warm-up shooting at full speed 3	7	★★
Equipment required:	2 cones, sufficient number of handballs		

Course:

- 1 starts without a ball, runs around the cone, and receives a pass from 2 into his running path (A).
- 4 starts a bit delayed, runs around the cone, and receives a pass from 5 into his running path (B).
- Afterwards, 2 starts, etc.

⚠ The players should time their action in such a way that there is a smooth rhythm for the goalkeeper.

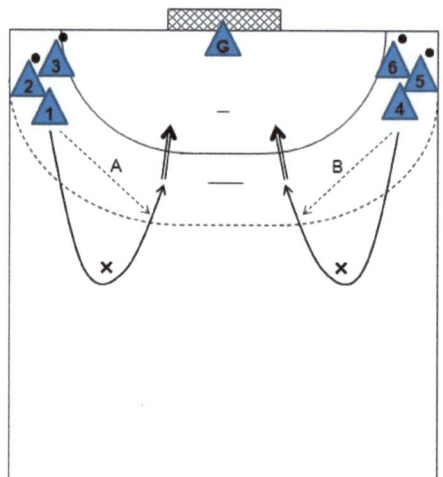

No. 35	Series of shots with a simple crossing move	7	★★
Equipment required:	Sufficient number of handballs		

Course:

- 1 starts and crosses with 2 (A) who dynamically runs a curve (B).
- 2 shoots at the goal at full speed and as instructed (hands, top, bottom, middle) (C).
- 1 moves backward to the initial position of 2 after the crossing (D).
- 3 starts and crosses with 1, etc.

Variant:
- Change sides.
- Quick jump shot (immediate shot, without delay in the air).

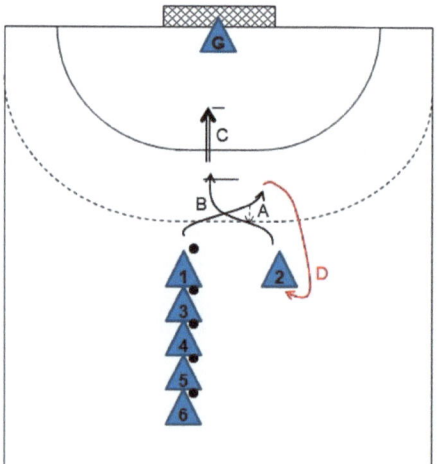

No. 36	Quick back and forth, shot from the left/right wing position 2	7	
Equipment required:	4 cones, sufficient number of handballs		

Course:

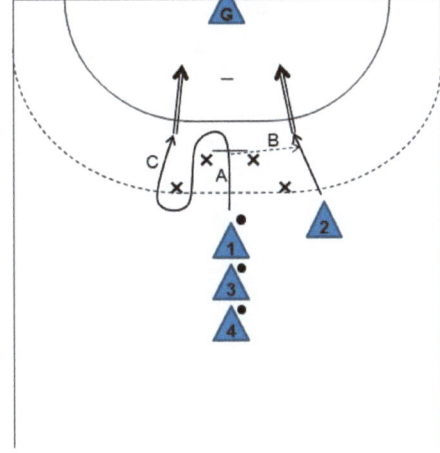

- 1 does a piston movement towards the gap between the cones (A) and passes (B) the ball to 2 who does a parallel piston movement, and shoots at the goal as instructed (top, middle, bottom), and from within the corridor (players on the right shoot at the right side of the goal, players on the left shoot at the left side of the goal).
- Afterwards, 1 takes three to four quick steps backward to the left and around the cone on the left, before immediately running forward again (C).
- 3 immediately does a piston movement once 1 has passed the ball to 2, and passes the ball to 1 on the left.
- Afterwards, the players start the course over on the right side.

Variants:
- Jump shot.
- Increase speed continuously.

⚠️ Dynamic back and forth movements.

No. 37	Warm-up shooting with crossing moves	9	★★
Equipment required:	3 cones, ball box with sufficient number of handballs		

Course:

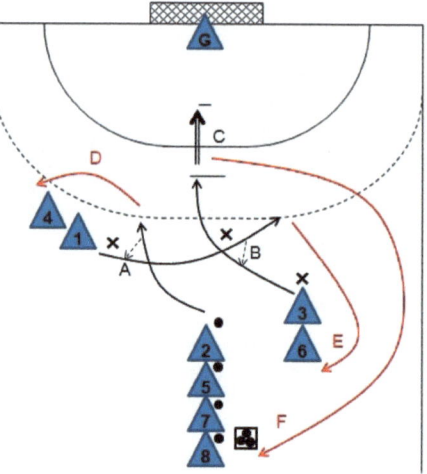

- 2 dynamically dribbles the ball to the left and crosses with 1 (A).
- 1 dynamically dribbles to the right, around the cone, and crosses with 3 (B).
- 3 approaches the goal and shoots as instructed (top, middle, bottom) (C).
- Following the action, the players line up again (D, E, and F; 3 fetches a new ball and lines up for the center back position).
- Afterwards, 5 starts and crosses with 4, etc.

Effective goalkeeper warm-up shooting
60 exercises for every handball training unit

No. 38	Series of shots with defense action	8	★★
Equipment required:	Sufficient number of handballs		

Course:

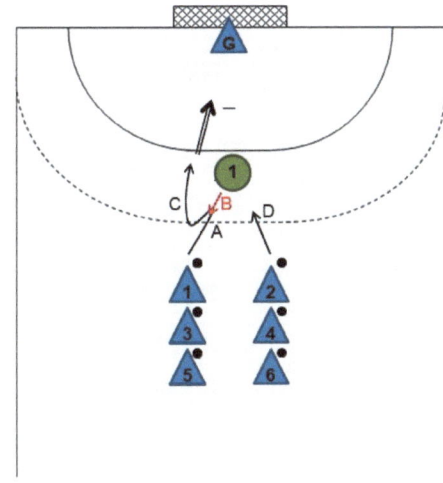

- ① starts to run with the ball and lifts his arm for a shot (A).
- ① dynamically steps forward towards ▲ and pushes him back in the usual defending manner (about half a meter) (B).
- ① moves back to his initial position after the action against ▲.
- After ▲ has been pushed back, he approaches the goal and shoots as instructed (hands, top, bottom, middle) (C).
- Now ② starts the same course on the other side (D).

⚠ Make sure that ① maintains the correct defense posture (attacking the throwing hand and the diagonal hip).

⚠ The players should give ① enough time so that he can move back to his initial position.

⚠ ① should push back the attacking player dynamically rather than tackling him.

No. 39	Series of shots with parallel piston movement and defense	9	★★
Equipment required:	2 cones, sufficient number of handballs		

Course:

- 3 starts the piston movement with a ball (A).
- 1 dynamically makes a step forward (B).
- 3 must pass the ball early enough (C) so that he is not interrupted by 1 (1 should clearly make a step forward towards 3, however).
- 2 receives a pass into his running path and shoots at the goal as instructed (hands, top, bottom, middle) (D) (to the left side from within the corridor).
- After his pass, 3 immediately moves back dynamically to his initial position (E).
- 1 dynamically moves backward and to the 6-meter line (F) in order to immediately make a step forward towards the piston movement path (G) of 4.
- 3 receives a pass into his running path and shoots at the goal as instructed (to the right side from within the corridor) (H).

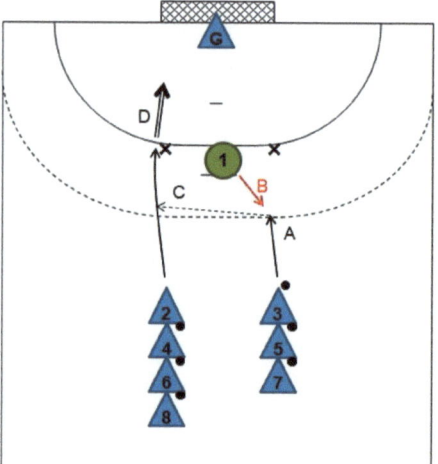

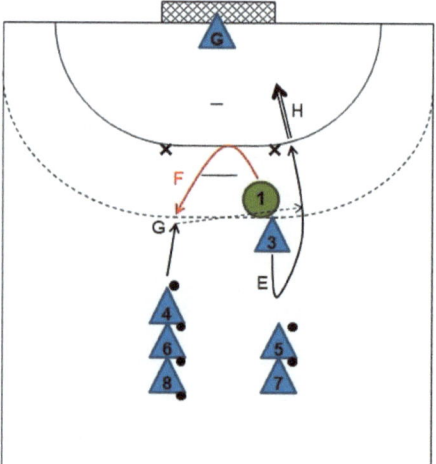

Variant:

- Jump shot.
- Shooting with the wrong foot in front.
- Sprinting to the center line immediately after the shot.

Effective goalkeeper warm-up shooting
60 exercises for every handball training unit

No. 40	Series of shots with piston movement/counter movement 1	9	★★
Equipment required:	2 cones, 2 bibs, sufficient number of handballs		

Course:

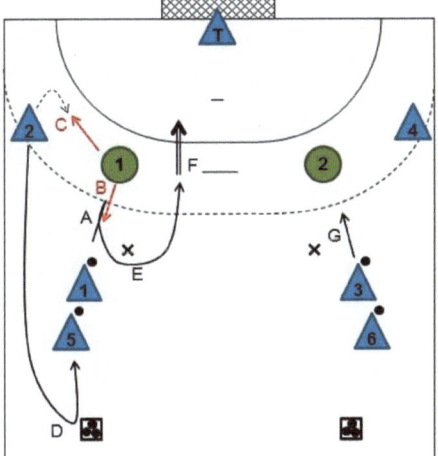

- 1 dynamically runs forward and lifts his arm for a shot (A).
- 1 defends by moving forward, attacking his opponent's throwing hand, and vigorously pushing 1 back (B).
- Immediately after the action, 2 throws a bib in the air. 1 must now try to catch the bib before it touches the ground (C).
- 2 sprints to the ball box, picks up a new ball and lines up again (D).
- 1 moves backward after the initial action, runs around the cone (E), and shoots at the goal as instructed (top, middle, bottom) (F).
- 1 becomes the new defense player, and 1 throws the bib in the air.
- A bit delayed, 3 starts the same course on the other side (G).

⚠ Make sure that 1 stands in the correct defense posture.

⚠ 1 should exert pressure with his body during the first action so that 1 is forced to push 1 back powerfully.

⚠ The bib should be thrown in such a way (C) that it is challenging for 1 to catch it just in time.

No. 41	Series of shots with piston movement/counter movement 2	7	
Equipment required:	4 cones, ball box with sufficient number of handballs		

Course:

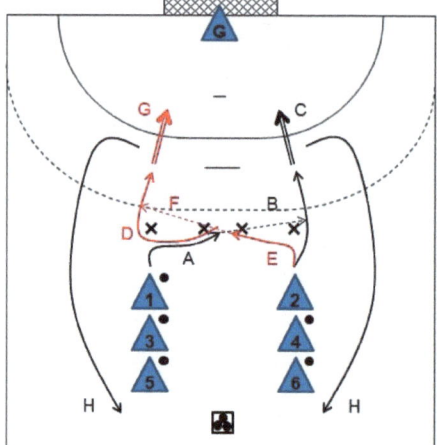

- 1 has a ball, does a dynamic piston movement forward, and then moves to the right (A).
- 2 starts a bit delayed, runs around the outmost cone and to the right, receives a pass from 1 into his running path (B), and shoots at the right side of the goal as instructed (hands, top, bottom, middle), and from within the corridor (C).
- Immediately after the pass from 1 to 2 (B), 1 moves back dynamically and runs around the cone on the left (D).
- As soon as 1 is moving to the side (D), 4 starts with a ball, does a dynamic piston movement forward, runs to the left (E), and passes the ball into the running path of 1 (F).
- 1 shoots at the goal as instructed and from within the corridor (G).
- After the shot (C and G), the players sprint to the ball box, pick up a new ball, and line up again (H).
- The players repeat the course until there is no ball left in the box.

No. 42	Series of shots with piston movement/counter movement 3	7	
Equipment required:	6 cones, sufficient number of handballs		

Course:

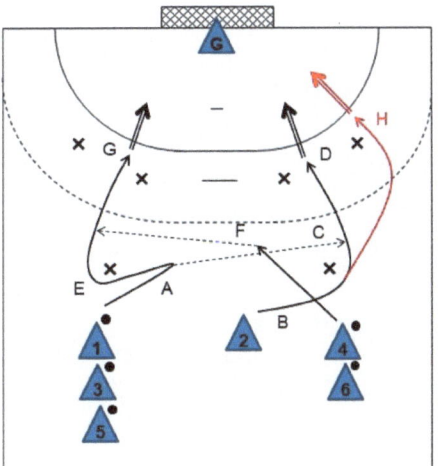

- **1** has a ball, does a dynamic piston movement towards the center (A), and passes the ball to **2** (C) who starts from the center (B).
- **2** shoots at the short corner goalpost as instructed (hands, top, bottom, middle) (D).
- After the pass (C), **1** immediately moves back dynamically, and runs around the cone (E). **4** does a dynamic piston movement towards the center and passes him the ball (F).
- **1** shoots at the short corner of the goal as instructed (top or bottom) (G).

Variant:
- The shooting player runs around the outmost cone and shoots at the goal (H).

⚠ The players should take the turn after the pass at high speed (E).

⚠ Make sure the players do the piston movement clearly and vigorously towards the center (F).

No. 43	Series of shots with additional task for the goalkeeper 1	7	★★
Equipment required:	1 small vaulting box, ball box with sufficient number of handballs		

Initial position:
- Position a small vaulting box on the goal line. The goalkeeper sits on the box, viewing direction towards the shooting players.

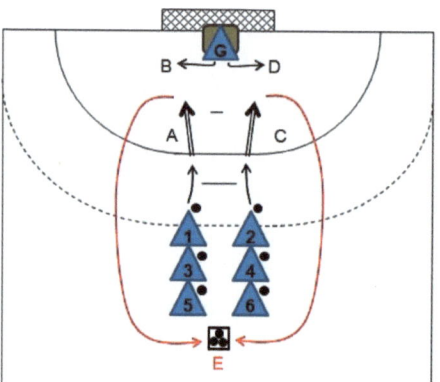

Course:
- 1 approaches the goal with the ball and shoots top (left) at the goal (A), from within the corridor.
- G gets up dynamically and tries to save the ball shot at the top of the goal (B).
- Afterwards, G sits down on the box again.
- As soon as G is sitting on the box again, 2 starts to approach the goal and shoots top (right) at the goal, from within the corridor (C).
- G gets up dynamically and tries to save the ball shot at the top of the goal (D).
- Afterwards, G sits down on the box again.
- And so on.
- After the shot, the shooting players dynamically sprint to the ball box, pick up a new ball, and line up again (E).

Series of shots:
- The players do 10 shots in a row. If a higher physical strain is desired for the goalkeeper, the players shoot more often (e.g. 20 times).
- The players shoot at the bottom of the goal, with and without the goalkeeper getting off the box with a hurdle jump.
- Diagonal series, top left – bottom right.
- Shooting a square, bottom left – top left – top right – bottom right, etc.

⚠ The goalkeeper should be given enough time to sit down.

⚠ Make sure the goalkeeper does the movement sequence correctly; the shooting players must adjust the speed in such a way that he is able to move in a proper and technically correct way!

⚠ The goalkeeper should be given sufficient resting time between the various series.

Effective goalkeeper warm-up shooting
60 exercises for every handball training unit

No. 44	Series of shots with additional task for the goalkeeper 2	7	★★
Equipment required:	1 balloon, ball box with sufficient number of handballs		

Basic setting:
- G should always start the action from the center of the goal.

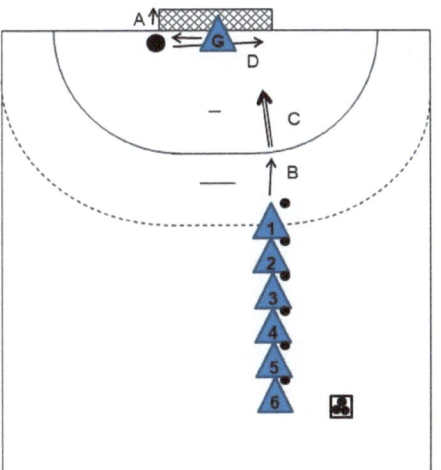

Course:
- G stands next to the goal and pushes a balloon in the air so that it flies upwards (A). Immediately afterwards, he goes back to the center of the goal.
- 1 has a ball, approaches the goal dynamically (B), and shoots as instructed (hands, top, bottom, middle) (C), as soon as G has returned to the center of the goal.
- G moves towards the respective corner and tries to save the shot (D).
- Immediately afterwards, G runs out of the goal in order to push the balloon in the air again (A).
- And so on.
- Once they have shot, the players sprint to the center line and quickly pick up their ball so that there are no long breaks in between the series of shots.

Extended shooting instructions:
- Top and bottom of the goal alternately.
- Change corners after approx. 10 shots.

⚠ The players should time their shots in such a way that there is a smooth rhythm for the goalkeeper. Moreover, the players should shoot in such a way that the goalkeeper is able to reach them; he should not have to wait for a shot, either.

⚠ must reach the balloon before it touches the ground.

Effective goalkeeper warm-up shooting
60 exercises for every handball training unit

No. 45	Series of shots with additional task for the goalkeeper 3	8	★★
Equipment required:	Ball box with sufficient number of handballs		

Basic setting:

- G1 should always start the action from the center of the goal.

Course:

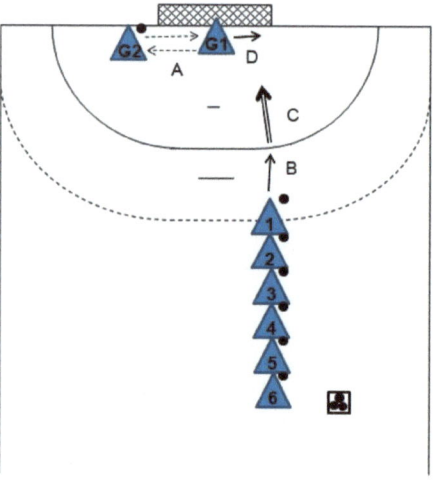

- G2 passes a ball to G1 who immediately plays a return pass (A).
- 1 has a ball, approaches the goal dynamically (B), and shoots at the right side of the goal as instructed (hands, top, bottom, middle) (C), as soon as G1 has returned to the center of the goal.
- G1 moves towards the respective corner and tries to save the shot (D).
- Afterwards, G1 moves back to the center of the goal and receives another pass from G2.
- And so on.

 The players should time their shots in such a way that there is a smooth rhythm for the goalkeeper. Moreover, the players should shoot in such a way that the goalkeeper is able to save the shots; he should not have to wait for a shot, either.

 Change the goalkeeper/corners after approx. 10 shots.

Extended shooting instructions:
- Top and bottom of the goal alternately.

Effective goalkeeper warm-up shooting
60 exercises for every handball training unit

No. 46	Series of shots with additional task for the goalkeeper 4	8	★★
Equipment required:	2 cones, ball box with sufficient number of handballs		

Course:

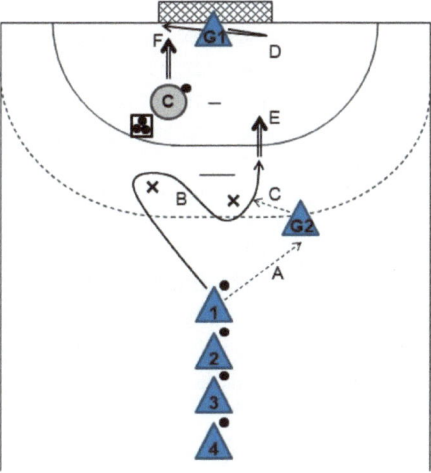

- **1** passes the ball to **G2** (A), runs around the two cones at high speed (B), and receives a return pass from **G2** (C).
- **G1** starts from the center of the goal and saves (D) the ball shot by **1** at the right side of the goal (E).
- Immediately after the action, **G1** sidesteps to the other goalpost and saves the ball shot by **c** at the left side of the goal (F).
- Immediately afterwards, **G1** moves back to his initial position in the center of the goal and waits for the next shot, etc.
- Repeat the course with the other shooting players until each player has shot once.
- Change the side from which the players shoot after 1 to 2 rounds.

⚠️ **G1** should start his action (D) from the center of the goal and not wait in the corner, at which **1** is about to shoot.

⚠️ Immediately after he has saved the first shot, **G1** should sidestep dynamically in order to also save the second shot (F).

No. 47	Series of shots with additional task for the goalkeeper 5	7	★★
Equipment required:	7 cones, 2 ball boxes with sufficient number of handballs		

Setting:
- Define the shooting positions with two cones on either side.
- Position three additional cones of different color for the goalkeeper (see figure).

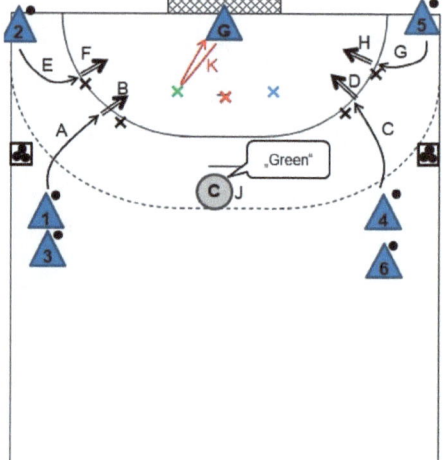

Course:
- 1 starts approaching the gap between the cones with a ball (A) and shoots at the left side of the goal as instructed (top, bottom) (B).
- Afterwards, 4 starts to approach the gap between the cones (C) and shoots at the right side of the goal as instructed (D).
- Subsequently, 2 shoots from the left wing position (E and F), and 5 shoots from the right wing position (G and H), as instructed.
- Afterwards, the coach calls out a color (J; here "green"), and the goalkeeper must touch the respective cone (K).
- Then the course starts over, with a shot from 3.

⚠ The players should shoot in such a way that the goalkeeper is forced to get in the right position quickly; he should be able to save the shots, however.

⚠ Immediately after the shot, the players must pick up a new ball from the box for the next round.

No. 48	Series of shots with additional task for the goalkeeper and the field players	7	★★
Equipment required:	2 small gym mats, 6 cones, sufficient number of handballs		

Preparation:
- Position 6-8 cones on the goal line, with a distance of about 2 meters between each cone.
- G does the course sidestepping (viewing direction towards the shooting players).
- Shooting instructions: top, middle, bottom.

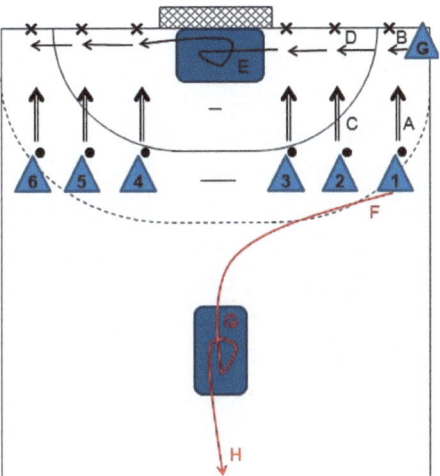

Course:
- G starts next to the side line.
- 1 stands at cone level and shoots (A) from this position, in such a way that G is able to save the ball while in motion (B).
- Afterwards, 2 shoots in such a way (C) that G is able to save the shot while smoothly moving on (D), etc.
- After the shot of 3, G quickly does a forward somersault on the mat. Following this, the players repeat the course until the last player (6) has shot.
- As soon as the players 1 to 6 have shot, they immediately start a counter movement (F), do a forward somersault on the mat (G), get up quickly, and sprint to the center line (H).

⚠ The players should shoot in such a way that G is able to move towards the cone at the right time and save the shot.

⚠ Make sure that the players adjust to the new situation immediately after they have shot, sprint to the mat, do the somersault, and then sprint to the center line.

Effective goalkeeper warm-up shooting
60 exercises for every handball training unit

No. 49	Series of shots with crossing moves and additional task for the goalkeeper	8	★★
Equipment required:	1 small gym mat, 2 cones, ball box with sufficient number of handballs		

Course:

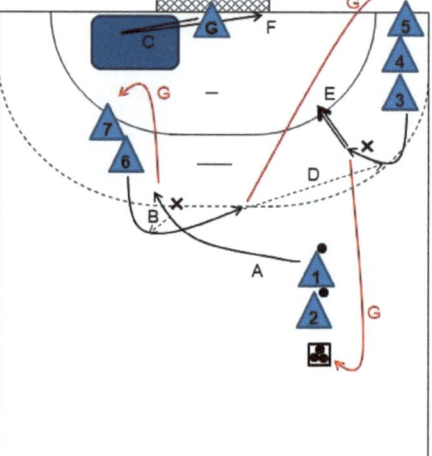

- 🔺1 has a ball and runs far to the left, next to the 7-meter line (A).
- 🔺6 starts at the 6-meter line and runs a curve, takes on the crossing of 🔺1 (B), and passes the ball into the running path of 🔺3 (D), who has started to approach the goal from the wing position.
- 🔺G starts from the center and runs to the small gym mat, where he does a somersault (C).
- 🔺3 runs around the cone and shoots at the right side of the goal as instructed (top, middle, bottom) (E).
- 🔺G moves back to the goal dynamically after the somersault (C) and tries to save (F) the ball shot by 🔺3 (E).
- Following the action, 🔺1, 🔺3, and 🔺6 line up at the next position, and the players repeat the course, etc.
- Change the side after a while.

⚠️ 🔺G should time his action (C and F) in such a way that he is able to perform a smooth move.

Effective goalkeeper warm-up shooting
60 exercises for every handball training unit

No. 50	Series of shots with dynamic running moves	7	★★
Equipment required:	4 cones, sufficient number of handballs		

Position for the first pass:

- ① stands between the cones, without a ball.

Course:

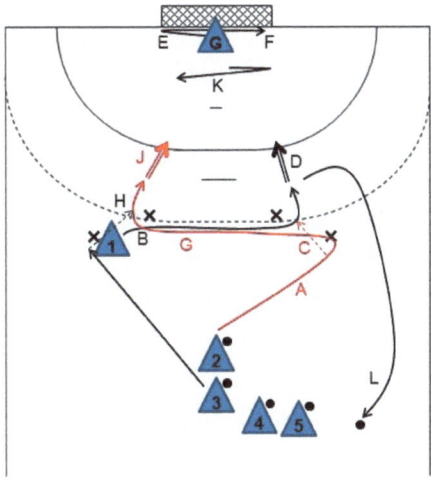

- ② has a ball and does a piston movement to the right, towards the cone (A).
- ① quickly sidesteps (B) along the 9-meter line (viewing direction towards the goal), receives a pass from ② (C), and shoots at the right side of the goal as instructed (hands, middle, bottom) (D).
- Ⓖ starts from the center of the goal, dynamically sidesteps to the left, touches the goalpost (E), dynamically sidesteps back, and saves (F) the ball shot by ① at the right side of the goal (D).
- ② runs along the 9-meter line immediately after passing the ball (C and G) (viewing direction towards the goal), receives a pass from ③ (H), and shoots at the left side of the goal as instructed (top, middle, bottom) (J).
- Ⓖ starts from the center of the goal, dynamically sidesteps to the right, touches the goalpost, dynamically sidesteps back, and saves (K) the ball shot by ② at the left side of the goal (J).
- And so on.
- ① picks up a new ball after his shot, and lines up immediately in order to play the pass to the last player.

⚠ Choose the distance between the cones in such a way that Ⓖ faces a series of shots and is able to do the running and saving moves in a technically correct manner.

⚠ When catching the ball, (C and H) the players should rotate their trunk towards the player passing the ball.

Effective goalkeeper warm-up shooting
60 exercises for every handball training unit

No. 51	Warm-up shooting for two goalkeepers at one goal	8	★★
Equipment required:	6 cones, sufficient number of handballs		

Course:

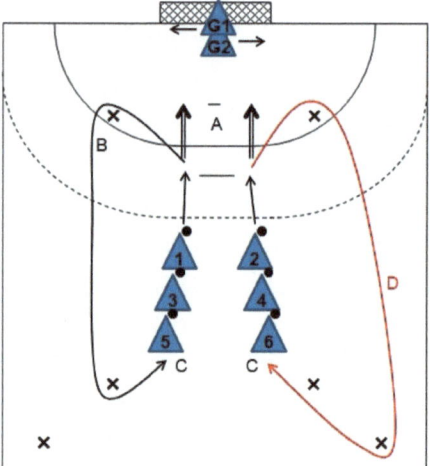

- 1 and 2 start their shooting actions in parallel. 1 shoots at the left side of the goal as instructed (hands, top, bottom, middle), from within the corridor; 2 shoots at the right side of the goal as instructed, from within the corridor.
- Both goalkeepers should start from the center of the goal. G1 saves the shot of 1, G2 saves the shot of 2.
- 3 and 4 start a bit delayed and shoot at the left and right side of the goal, respectively, in order to create a smooth rhythm for the goalkeepers.
- The goalkeepers change sides and now save the shots at the respective other side of the goal; i.e. G1 saves the shot of 4, and G2 saves the shot of 3.
- Once they have shot, 1 and 2 sprint around the cones (B), pick up another ball, and line up for the next round (C).
- And so on.

Variant:
- If a player fails to shoot as instructed, he must sprint the longer way (D).

No. 52	Saving banana shots and initiating fast breaks	10	★★
Equipment required:	Sufficient number of handballs		

Setting:
- The players line up at the 6-meter line, each holding a handball. They hold their handball in such a way that the goalkeeper can reach it.

Course:
- G1 starts at the goalpost and sprints to 1 who holds his handball in front of him, in a position reachable for G1 (A).
- G1 touches the ball with one hand and immediately sprints back to the goal. 1 now shoots a banana shot, and G1 tries to reach the ball and save it (B).
- 1 starts a fast break immediately after the banana shot (C), receives a pass from G1 into his running path (D), and eventually shoots at the goal (E).
- After initiating the fast break (D), G1 runs back to the goalpost, touches it, and repeats the course with 2.
- And so on.

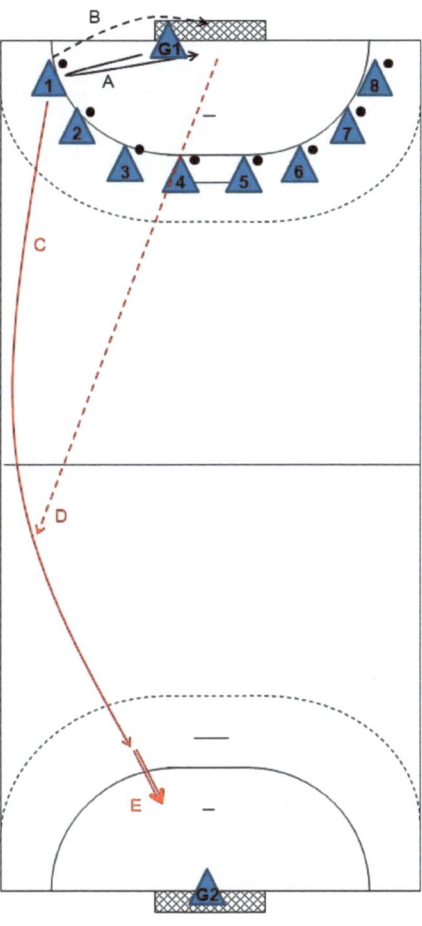

No. 53	Series of shots and fast break initiation with coordination exercise	8	★★
Equipment required:	7 cones, 10 hoops, ball box with sufficient number of handballs (2 balls per player)		

Course:
- 1 starts with a ball, runs dynamically back and forth (viewing direction always towards the goal line) from cone to cone (A), and eventually shoots at the goal as instructed (top, middle, bottom) (B).
- After the shot, 1 immediately runs around the cone and through the line of hoops as instructed (C).
- As soon as he has run through the line of hoops, G2 plays a long pass to 1 (D) who increases his speed considerably.
- 1 sprints to the 6-meter line, steps into the goal zone with one foot (E), sprints back to his group, and lines up again (F).
- Each player must shoot 2-3 times.

Instructions for running though the line of hoops:
- One step per hoop, running through the line as fast as possible.
- Two steps per hoop (left and right foot).
- Jumping with the left/right foot.
- Jumping with both feet.

Variants:
- Sidestepping from cone to cone.
- Shooting with the wrong foot in front.

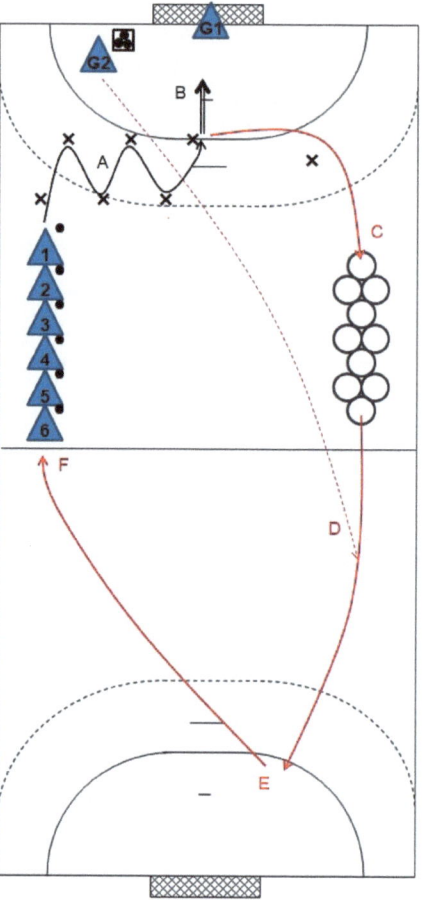

Effective goalkeeper warm-up shooting
60 exercises for every handball training unit

No. 54	Fast break initiation plus series of shots	10	★★
Equipment required:	2 cones, sufficient number of handballs		

Course:

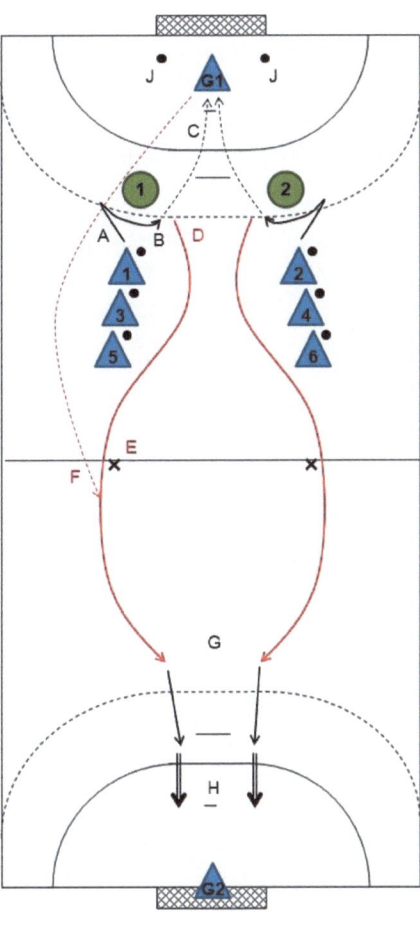

- ① makes three steps (without dribbling) vigorously to the left (A).
- ① then dynamically dribbles to the right (B) and plays a jump shot pass to the goalkeeper (G1) (C).
- After the pass (C), ① immediately starts a fast break (D), runs around the cone at the center line (E), and receives a pass from the goalkeeper (G1) into his running path (F).
- ② starts the course a bit later than ① so that he does not have to wait before playing the jump shot pass.
- And so on.
- ① and ② wait in the other half of the court (G) until 5-6 players have arrived. Now they begin the warm-up shooting (H) for the second goalkeeper (G2) as instructed (top, middle, bottom).
- ① and ② should also do the sidestep moves and offer some resistance, but allow the pass to the goalkeeper. After their last action, they also start a fast break and each receive a pass from the goalkeeper (who uses the balls lying next to the goal) (J).
- Following this, the players repeat the course towards the first goal, etc.

Effective goalkeeper warm-up shooting
60 exercises for every handball training unit

No. 55	Series of 4 shots with subsequent fast break 1	8	★★
Equipment required:	Ball box with sufficient number of handballs		

Setting:

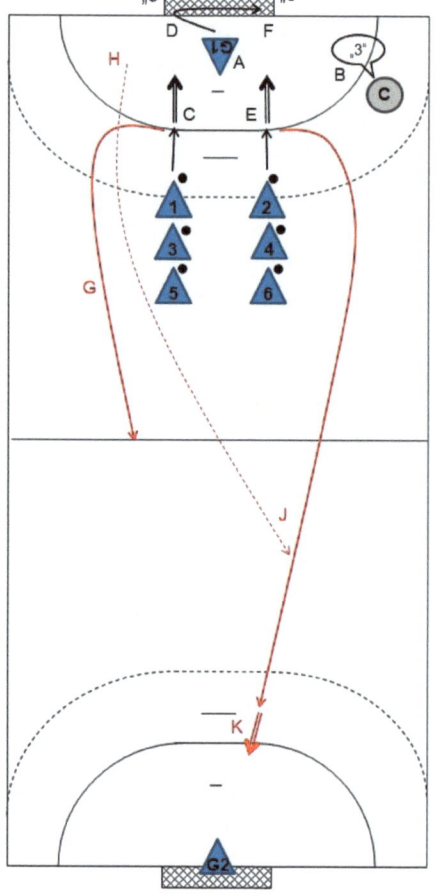

- G1 stands with his back turned at the players.
- The players need to shoot a series of 4 shots sticking to the following rules: If C calls out an uneven number while G1 is doing jumping jacks:
    - 1st player shoots top left.
    - 2nd player shoots top right.
    - 3rd player shoots bottom left.
    - 4th player shoots bottom right.
- If C calls out an even number, the course is to be done the other way round:
    - 1st player shoots top right.
    - 2nd player shoots top left, etc.
- The players also need to pay attention to the number the coach calls out and start accordingly:
    - Uneven number: 1 starts.
    - Even number: 2 starts.

Course:

- G1 does fast jumping jacks (A) on the spot.
- C calls out a number ("3" in the example).
- This is the sign for G1 to turn around at once and to get in position in the goal as well as for 1 to start the series of shots top left (C).
- G1 tries to save the 1st ball (top left) (D).
- 2 starts a bit delayed and shoots top right (E).
- G1 sidesteps and tries to save the ball (F).
- 3 starts a bit delayed and shoots bottom left.

- At the end, 4 shoots bottom right.
- After they have shot, 1, 2, and 3 sprint to the center line at once (G).
- 4 immediately starts a fast break after his shot, receives a long pass from G1 (J), and shoots at the goal on the other side of the court (K).
- Afterwards, it's the next four players' turn.

⚠ The goalkeeper G1 should be in a good throwing position before throwing the long pass. His position should allow him to play a diagonal pass (H), since, for 4, a diagonal pass is easier to catch.

Variant:
- Set calculation tasks for the shooting, e.g., "5 plus 8".

Effective goalkeeper warm-up shooting
60 exercises for every handball training unit

No. 56	Series of 4 shots with subsequent fast break 2	8	★★
Equipment required:	Ball box with sufficient number of handballs		

Course:

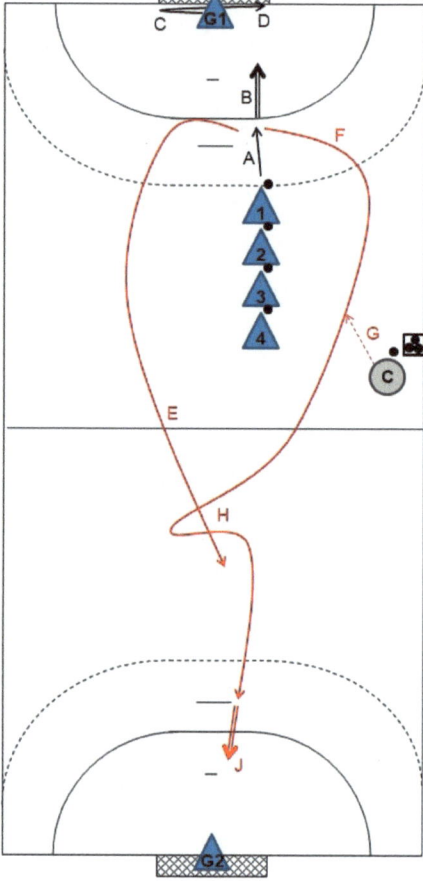

- **1** starts with a ball (A) and shoots top right (B).
- **G1** starts from the center of the goal, dynamically sidesteps to the left, touches the goalpost (C), dynamically sidesteps back, and saves (D) the ball shot by **1** top right (B).
- After each shot, **G1** must move back to the center of the goal.
- **2** starts the same course a bit delayed and also shoots top right.
- **G1** repeats the course (C and D) in order to save the ball shot by **2**.
- Once he has shot (B), **1** immediately starts a counter movement and runs to the other half of the court (E). **2** starts a fast break immediately after his shot (F), and receives a pass from **C** into his running path (G).
- **2** now plays 1-on-1 against **1** (H), and eventually shoots at the goal (J).

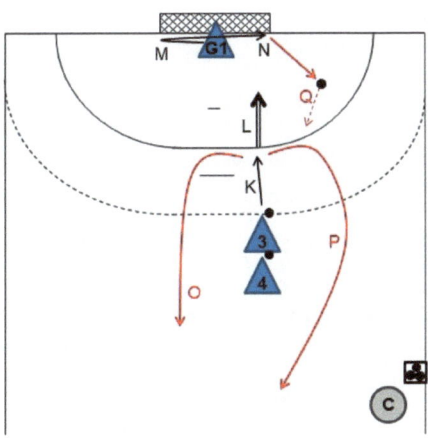

- Following the shot of 2, 3 and 4 start the same course a bit delayed (K and L) in order to create a series of four shots for G1 (C, D, M, and N).
- Once he has shot (L), 3 immediately starts a counter movement and runs to the other half of the court (O).
- 4 immediately starts a fast break after his shot (P) and receives a pass from G1 into his running path (Q).
- 4 now plays 1-on-1 against 3 and eventually shoots at the goal.
- Afterwards, repeat the course with the next four attacking players.
- Change the shooting side and instructions (top, middle, bottom) after a few series.

⚠ The players should shoot in such a way that G1 has enough time to sidestep to the goalpost and back (C and D or M and N) in a proper and dynamic manner.

No. 57	Warm-up shooting at full speed 4	8	★★★
Equipment required:	4 cones, sufficient number of handballs		

Course:

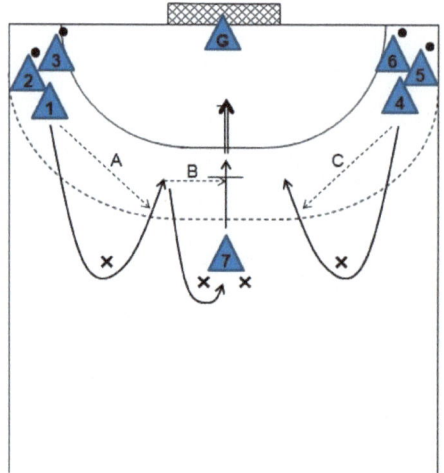

- 1 starts without a ball, runs around the cone, and receives a pass from 2 into his running path (A).
- 1 does a piston movement and passes the ball into the running path of 7 who shoots at the goal as instructed (top, middle, bottom) (B).
- 1 immediately moves backward after passing the ball to 7 and runs through the cone goal in the center.
- 4 starts a bit delayed, runs around the cone, and receives a pass from 5 into his running path (C).
- 4 does a piston movement and passes the ball into the running path of 1 who shoots at the goal.
- And so on.

⚠ The players should time their action in such a way that there is a smooth rhythm for the goalkeeper.

Effective goalkeeper warm-up shooting
60 exercises for every handball training unit

No. 58	Series of shots with piston movement/counter movement 4	7	★★★
Equipment required:	2 small gym mats, 2 cones, sufficient number of handballs		

Course:

- **1** does a dynamic three-step piston movement (without dribbling) (A) with a shooting feint (shoulder rotated, throwing hand in the air, foot planted firmly on the floor).
- **1** takes a turn backward, dynamically dribbles around the mat and towards the inner side (B).
- **2** does a dynamic running feint (C) and receives a pass from **1** into his running path (D).
- **2** shoots at the short corner goalpost as instructed (hands, top, bottom) (E).
- After the pass from **1** (D), **4** does a dynamic three-step piston movement with a shooting feint (F). Afterwards, he takes a turn, runs around the mat, and passes the ball to **1** (H), who has run a curve around the mat (G), and eventually shoots at the goal (at the short corner goalpost as instructed) (K).
- As soon as **4** passed the ball, **3** immediately starts the piston movement (J), etc.

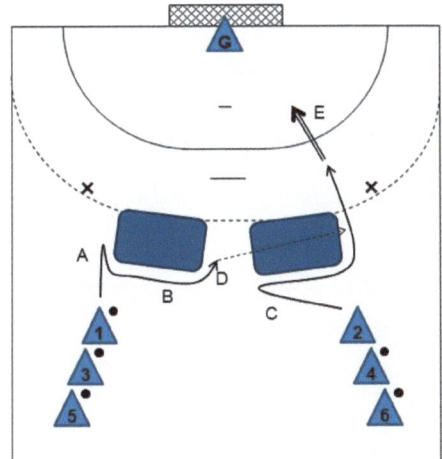

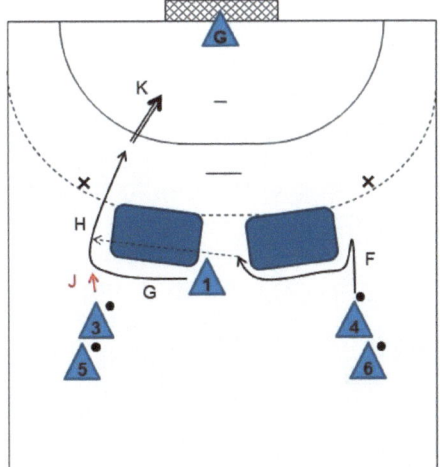

⚠ When starting the piston movement, the players should stand as close to the mat that they need to do three steps only, but nevertheless can do a vigorous piston movement towards the side of the mat.

No. 59	Series of shots with coordination exercise for goalkeepers and field players	8	★★★
Equipment required:	4 small vaulting boxes, 10 cones, small gym mat, 2 ball boxes with sufficient number of handballs		

Course:

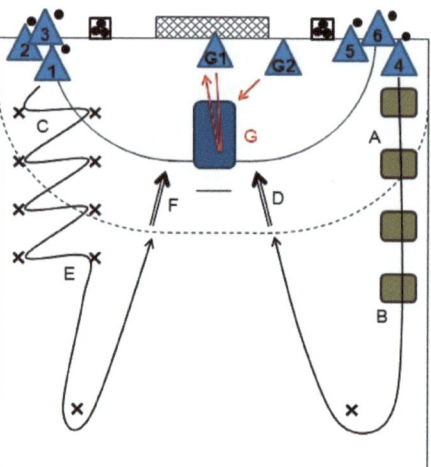

- 4 has a ball, jumps on the first small vaulting box with both feet, down between the two boxes with both feet, on the second box with both feet, and so on (A).
- As soon as 4 has finished (B), 1 starts with a ball and sidesteps through the cones (defense posture, holding his arms (with ball) above the head) (C).
- 4 runs around the cone and dynamically approaches the goal in order to shoot a jump shot (D).
- As soon as 1 has finished the cone course exercise (E), 5 starts to jump over the small vaulting boxes.
- 1 runs around the cone and dynamically approaches the goal in order to shoot a jump shot (F).
- And so on.

Course (intermediate exercise) for the goalkeepers:
- Before each shot, the goalkeepers do a somersault on the gym mat (G) and then quickly run to the goal to save the shot. The goalkeepers change after each action.

Variants for the shooting players:
- Stem shot.
- The players do a jump shot, but jump with the wrong foot.

Variants for the goalkeepers:
- Somersault variants -> forward, backward, to the side.
- Turn wheels.
- Sit down and get up quickly.

Overall course:
- Each player performs 10 actions (shots); afterwards, allow a short break and add more rounds, as necessary.

Effective goalkeeper warm-up shooting
60 exercises for every handball training unit

No. 60	Series of shots with subsequent fast break initiation	7	★★★
Equipment required:	Sufficient number of handballs		

Basic course:
- Four players do the course.
- 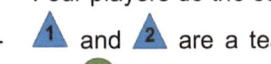 and are a team, and and are a team.
- Put a spare ball next to the goal which G may use if the other balls have rolled away.

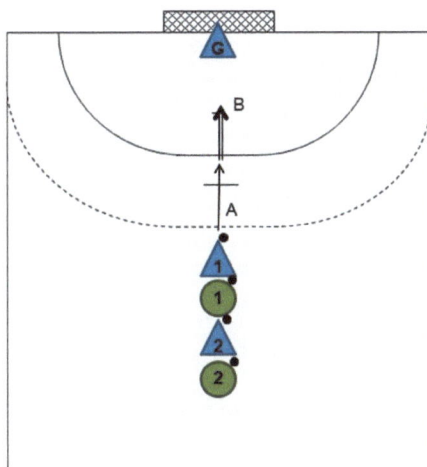

Shooting sequence:
- 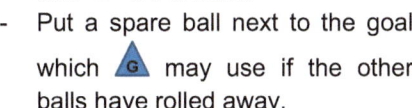 shoots bottom left.
- 1 shoots top right.
- 2 shoots top left.
- 2 shoots bottom right.

Course:
- 1 starts (A) and shoots at the goal as instructed (bottom left) (B).
- 1 and 2 each start a bit delayed and also shoot as instructed.
- Once they have shot, the players move to the side, but stay inside the 9-meter zone and wait for 2 to do the last shot.

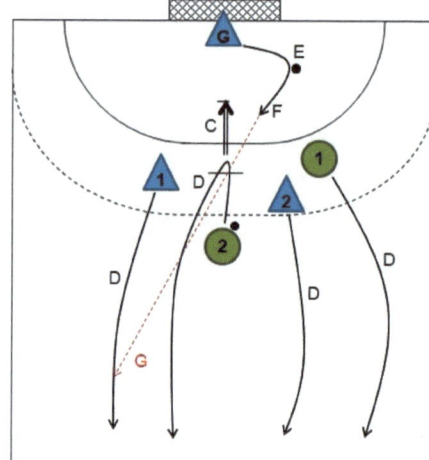

- ② also starts and shoots as instructed (C).
- The last shot is the sign for ▲1, ▲2, ①, and ② to start the subsequent action – a fast break (D).
- As fast as possible, ▲G fetches one of the four balls shot at the goal (E) and initiates the fast break. He may freely choose the player who will receive his pass (G) (▲1 in the example).
- ▲1 and ▲2 now play 2-on-2 against ① and ② on the goal in the other half of the court.
- If ① or ② win the ball, they may try to score a goal themselves.
- The team which has scored a goal wins. The losing team must do five push-ups, for example. If none of the teams has scored a goal, all four players must do five push-ups.

Variant:
- ▲G must play the pass (G) before the players have crossed the center line.

About the editor

JÖRG MADINGER, born in Heidelberg (Germany) in 1970

July 2014 (further training): 3-day coaching workshop: "Basic components of goalkeeper training", held by the **German Handball Association (Deutscher Handballbund, DHB)**
Lecturers: Michael Neuhaus, Renate Schubert, Marco Stange, Norbert Potthoff, Olaf Gritz, Andreas Thiel, Henning Fritz

May 2014 (further training): 3-day coaching further training during the VELUX EHF Final4, held by the **German Handball Coaching Association (Deutsche Handball Trainer Vereinigung, DHTV)/DHB**
Lecturers: Jochen Beppler (DHB coach), Christian vom Dorff (DHB referee), Mark Dragunski (coach of TuSeM Essen, Germany), Klaus-Dieter Petersen (DHB coach), Manolo Cadenas (coach of the Spanish national team)

May 2013 (further training): 3-day coaching further training during the VELUX EHF Final4, held by the **DHTV/DHB**
Lecturers: Prof. Dr. Carmen Borggrefe (University of Stuttgart, Germany), Klaus-Dieter Petersen (DHB coach), Dr. Georg Froese (sports psychologist), Jochen Beppler (DHB base camp coach), Carsten Alisch (young talents' hockey coach)

Since July 2012: A-License, DHB

Since February 2011: Handball club trainings, coaching (training and competitive areas)

November 2011: Foundation of the Handball Specialist Publishing Company (Handball Fachverlag) (handall-uebungen.de, Handball Practice and Special Handball Practice)

May 2009: Foundation of the handball online platform handball-uebungen.de

2008-2010: Youth coordinator and youth coach, SG Leutershausen (Germany)

Since 2006: B-License

Editor's note
In 1995, a friend convinced me to join him in coaching a handball youth team (male, under 13 years of age).

This was the beginning of my career as a team handball coach. Ever since I enjoyed working as a coach and had high requirements concerning my exercises. Soon, the standard pool of exercises wasn't enough for me anymore and I started to modify and develop drills myself.

Today, I coach a broad range of youth and adult teams with different performance levels and adjust my training units to the individual needs of the teams.

A few years ago, I started selling my exercises and drills online at handball-uebungen.de. Since, in handball training, there is a tendency towards a general athletic training that focuses on coordination work – especially in the training of youth teams –, a large number of my games and exercises can be applied to other sports as well.

Get inspired by the various game concepts, be creative, and rely on your own experiences!

Yours sincerely,
Jörg Madinger

Further reference books published by DV Concept

From warm-up to handball team play – 75 exercises for every handball training unit

By making your training units more diverse, you can increase the players' motivation, since you consistently offer new approaches to improve and refine familiar movement sequences. In this book, you will find inspiring exercises you can apply during each phase of your everyday team handball training – from warm-up and goalkeeper warm-up shooting to the common contents of the main phase and the closing games. Each exercise is illustrated and described in an easy, comprehensible manner. Specific notes give you tips on what you need to be aware of.

This book deals with the following key subjects:

Warm-up:
- Basic warm-up
- Short warm-up games
- Sprint contests
- Coordination
- Ball familiarization
- Goalkeeper warm-up shooting

Basic exercises, basic play, and target play:
- Offense/series of shots
- General offense
- Fast throw-off
- 1st and 2nd wave
- Defensive action
- Closing games
- Endurance

At the end of this book, you will find an entire methodological training unit. The objective of this training unit is to improve shooting and quick decision-making under pressure.

Minihandball training and handball training for young kids (5 training units)

Minihandball training and handball training for kids is different from handball training for older players and considerably different from handball training for competitive players. During their first contact with "handball", kids should be familiarized with the ball in a playful way. They should be taught that being active, doing sports, playing together, and even playing against each other is fun.

This book contains a short introduction to handball for kids and young children and its special characteristics as well as example exercises which help to make your training units interesting and more diverse.

Following this, there are five complete training units of different difficulty levels that focus on the basic handball techniques (dribbling, passing, catching, shooting, and defending in a game with opponents). The kids are playfully introduced to the subsequent handball-specific basics. At the same time, particular attention is payed to general physical experience and the development of coordination skills.

The exercises are illustrated and described in an easy, comprehensible manner. They can be immediately integrated in every training unit. By using the given training variants, you can easily adjust the difficulty level of the training units to the respective target group. The variants should also encourage you to modify and further develop the exercises to make each training unit a new and more diverse experience for the children.

Passing and catching while moving – 60 exercises for each handball training unit

Passing and catching are two basic handball techniques which must be trained and improved continuously. These 60 practical exercises offer you various options to train passing and catching in a challenging and diverse manner. The exercises particularly focus on improving passing and catching skills even during highly dynamic movements. The drills therefore combine new running paths and movements similar to real game situations.

The exercises are illustrated and described in an easy, comprehensible manner. They can be immediately integrated in every training unit. Various difficulty and complexity levels allow for adjustment of the passing and catching drills to each age group.

Competitive games for your everyday handball training – 60 exercises for each age-group

Handball needs quick and correct decisions in each game situation. This can be trained playfully and diversely through handball-specific games. These 60 exercises are divided into seven categories and train the playing skills.

The book deals with the following subjects:
- Team ball variants
- Team play with different targets
- Tag games
- Sprint and relay race games
- Ball throwing and transportation games
- Games from other types of sports
- Complex closing game variants

The exercises are illustrated and described in an easy, comprehensible manner. They can be immediately integrated in every training unit. Various difficulty levels, additional notes, and possible variations allow for adjustment to each age group.

Paperback from the Handball Practice series (Handball Praxis) (five training units each)

Handball Practice 11 – Extensive and diverse athletics training

Handball Practice 14 – Interaction of back position players with the pivot – Shifting, Screening, and Using the Russian Screen

For further reference and e-books visit us at:
www.handball-uebungen.de

www.ingramcontent.com/pod-product-compliance
Lightning Source LLC
Chambersburg PA
CBHW041803160426
43191CB00001B/24